Levitate
The Primate

Handjobs, Internet Dating,
and Other Issues for Men

Levitate
The Primate

Handjobs, Internet Dating,
and Other Issues for Men

Michael Thomsen

Winchester, UK
Washington, USA

First published by Zero Books, 2012
Zero Books is an imprint of John Hunt Publishing Ltd., Laurel House, Station Approach,
Alresford, Hants, SO24 9JH, UK
office1@jhpbooks.net
www.johnhuntpublishing.com
www.zero-books.net

For distributor details and how to order please visit the 'Ordering' section on our website.

Text copyright: Michael Thomsen 2011

ISBN: 978 1 78099 498 7

A CIP catalogue record for this book is available from the British Library.

Design: Stuart Davies

Printed and bound by CPI Group (UK) Ltd, Croydon, CR0 4YY

We operate a distinctive and ethical publishing philosophy in all
areas of our business, from our global network of authors to
production and worldwide distribution.

CONTENTS

For N,
for as long as I'm here.

Let me look at my demon objectively.
Vladimir Nabokov

... to hope till Hope creates
From its own wreck the thing it contemplates.
Percy Bysshe Shelley

Introduction & Mea Culpa

Revisiting old writing sometimes feels like rubbing a kitten's nose in its own shit after having failed to use the litter box. It's a masochistic comparison, but it fits. How easily do writers let the secret slip when referring to their own work – I've got some new shit that I'd really like to show you. I think it's a big improvement on my old shit. You might say 'stuff' or 'pieces' instead, but the implication is the same. I've excreted some things. Here, take a look. There's a superstitious sense of wrongness about recollecting a body of work, then, the haunted sloughing of all one's former selves. These thoughts couldn't quite be digested and instead needed to be expelled.

Sex is the optimum subject for writing because it too enters our lives on a spooky cloud of ritual, with rules it seems like we should already know. 'Am I doing this right?' I remember thinking when I asked a girl called Jill in my 6th Grade class to go to the movies with me. Years later, there is enough experience of rightness and wrongness to answer that question for myself, but the impulse to ask the question – to suspect myself – remains.

Many of these essays were written between 2008 and 2010, the majority of which were published on the website Nerve. They were not intended to tell a story at the time, but it's now clear that they do. These essays began as an attempt to make conversational potpourri about sex to ensnare the idle eyes of office workers in search of relief from spreadsheets and emails.

As I wrote, I wanted only to write about one thing, a woman I'd had a 2-month affair with and who had just moved to New York. She told me never to write about her, and looking back on these essays it's clear she was the subject of all them. The effect, in aggregate, is one of tacking against the wind, aiming in one direction while an invisible but palpable force is pushing in another.

In trying to write about everything but her, I wound up in strange territory on almost every occasion – sometimes a love song, sometimes a philosophy of handjobs. And so this corpus of memory and confession is a story straining to invent a purpose for itself other than the one it is finally, inescapably bound to tell. The disordered struggle is broken by the glimmers of light that come when the woman I love more than anyone else merges with the labor I love more than any other.

The remainder is a chaos of unhinged ideas that orbit around my sexual imagination in a time when porn can be seen on cell phones and the fear that one's worst secrets can be seen by anyone interested enough to write a name into an internet search field. So much shit comes up, after all, when you hit the search button. Here is some of mine.

Must Be Willing to Lie About How We Met

I've noticed that many of the women who date online prominently require their potential suitors to be willing to lie about how they met. Dating is embarrassing, especially when you've got to pitch your best romantic qualities to an anonymous rabble using only a series of Rorschach questionnaires and a thoroughly censored handful of photographs. It's alarmingly shameful to encounter these demands, admonishing any future intimate to never reveal you once stooped so low as to advertise the otherwise quite discriminating charms of yourself as a lover over the internet. Why would a woman want a partner to be an accomplice to her shame?

I first considered the idea of online dating at a friend's wedding in 2006, where I was surprised to learn, over toasts and dirty asides about the moral flexibility of certain bridesmaids, that most of my male friends had started dating online. In my early 20s I'd never considered the internet as a necessary tool for meeting people. There's something magical about the dating life during this period. You don't need to send winks and come up with clever email one-liners to disincarnate phantoms, and instead allow your minimally employed friends to talk you into going to the neighborhood bar on a Wednesday night, inadvertently drink four shots of tequila, and, by the time network television has shifted to infomercials, you're naked in a strange new bed.

Dating online should ideally be a less stressful and more efficient way for a man to go about meeting people. You don't have to fret about approach anxiety or competition with other lurking mammals in the proximate range of your beloved. You only just put up a metaphysical storefront that says what kind of television shows you like and those interested will respond. Instead of a night out oozing money on drinks and tossing

3

around one-liners to women in bars, you can send out ten come-ons in ten minutes. If men are doomed to be the formal pursuers, then online dating does for their needs what the advent of the computer did for secretaries.

Women are not, by culture and habit, pursuers – or rather the things they're regularly inclined to pursue are quite different than the fleshy suggestions that incite a man's curiosity to take a few steps forward. I imagine for many women – the upper-class, over-thirty group, judging by the demographic of people who've listed this particular requirement on their profiles – there's some social vertigo in acknowledging their availability. Knowing that you're pursuable must be a fantastic boon for the ego, and, likewise, there must be a bitter vulgarity in having to solicit pursuit as age sets in and more of your peers begin to disappear into the quicksand of marriage.

I don't see why meeting someone online should be any more or less embarrassing than meeting someone after four shots of tequila. The world is a big and overwhelming place and there's no need to feel ashamed about the impulse to find compan-ionship with someone outside of the normal grasp of your own social circle or visible surroundings. All the stories of how people first met wind up being silly and innocuous in the first place. You meet someone by accident or through some carefully crafted sequence of pick-up lines, then decide you want to spend more time with that person. Feeling embarrassed about having met online is like feeling embarrassed about the line your partner used on you the first time you met.

I remember the first time I met N. We met through friends and wound up spending a whole day together until we finally found ourselves alone in a deserted corner disco on a Sunday night. I knew from the second I saw her earlier in the day – I knew something. What is it, exactly, that happens when you see someone's face the first time? Love is an inadequate description here. Love is a practice of giving over time, not an encounter with a face. She seemed instantly familiar before she even turned around. 'Oh,' I thought to myself as I saw her back and shoulders, her whirling brown hair pinned in loose bun atop her head, held in place by a big pink flower. 'There you are.' It wasn't those words that were in my brain, but their shape, the way one feels a glove from the inside, knowing by touch the shape of the thing that surrounds the hand.

We spent the rest of the day trapped in a rictus of small talk. I remember at one point sitting next to her on a couch with a People magazine and wondering how I was going to come up with something interesting to say about a random celebrities caught leaving Starbucks without makeup. How are you supposed to be honest and intimate with someone who is, objectively, still a stranger? I slid across the surface of our conversation like a foal on ice.

Then we wound up sitting on a long vinyl bench against a wall, staring at a red and silver strobe light as it bounced off a disco ball and intermittently lit up the empty cement dance floor in front of us. A Motown song was playing. She asked me if I believed in theme songs, and said that if she had one for her life this would be it ('Is this a line,' I wondered). I told her my favorite song, which I decided when I was nineteen should be played at my funeral, is 'This Must Be the Place (Naïve Melody)' by the Talking Heads. She nodded. I wondered if she knew the song. No one under 30 knows that song, at least not by name.

I looked at her. I was terrified. We had been drinking all day, but I was sober now and adrenaline was making my body feel like a slowly inflating helium balloon. I tried to catch her eye, but she looked down again when she saw me looking. I looked away too, my palms breaking into a cold sweat. It wasn't the idea of rejection that was so scary. I was dizzy because I sensed this was the last moment I would look at her without anything else between us. These were the last few seconds without expectations, semantics, complications, or heartache. This was an embarkation point, a blind leap onto a vessel whose course was unknowable. 'There you are,' I thought. 'It's you.'

I looked back at her. She leaned toward me and half raised her head from her lap. The music had changed, it was all bass and silver lights across the coarse cement and cheap vinyl. Then we kissed.

Monogamy is for Losers

I was arguing with a married friend at a bar one weekend when I found myself blurting out, 'I could be in an open relationship.' I wasn't expecting that statement to come storming out of my mouth. It's something that sounds like it could be true. But I'm not really sure if I could manage it without imploding, and so I said it as if it were true. Earlier that week N had set her internet chat status as 'Monogamy is for quitters.' She'd been in New York for close to a year, and had just broken up with someone. She'd already committed to moving when I met her the year earlier and our affair lasted only two months before she left.

I've never felt a need to sleep with someone else while in a relationship. I don't think I would begrudge a partner for having those feelings. It's impossible to distill sex down to any one thing. It's intimacy and love. It's athletic silliness. It's indulgence and pleasure. It's something new every time. Even when the form and rhythm becomes repetitive there is something new happening. It doesn't always point to good things, but every encounter is particular and irreplaceably its own.

When I think about it rhetorically, the idea of a girlfriend wanting to sleep with another man seems fine. If sex is the proverbial glass of water, an act of physical exuberance and exploration, then there's nothing at all threatening about a girlfriend sleeping with someone else. Statistics suggest a huge percentage of people, close to half depending on whose study you believe, cheat during long-term relationships. It's shocking, but then I think of all of my friends – with their own uniquely repetitive infidelities – and it doesn't seem so improbable. Close to half of them have cheated on their partners at one time or another.

Most of those were random one-night encounters and not the drawn out affairs we secretly fear will be the end of us all. It was sex in the moment. Drunk and alone for a night, flushed with body and feeling, they decided to indulge themselves with some new stranger or a secret crush. Thinking about sex in those terms makes it seem like a body function. It's not pissing or shitting. It's a deep urge for affection and physical expression and little more than that. In that rhetorical vacuum, monogamy seems like a product of insecurity and antiquated social norms.

But the more I think about it in specific terms, relative to real women that I've dated, the more squeamish I become because I don't think I could cheat on someone else. I am probably monogamous to a fault. I'm single-minded in the same way that a dog is. There's only one voice that cuts through the rabble, one smell that pulls me away from a momentary curiosity. One hand whose touch settles me instantly.

A few years after I graduated from college I went home for Christmas. On Christmas Eve I went downtown with my parents to an old Spanish hotel that had stood in their town for almost a hundred years. Every year it was lit up with thousands of small lights, poinsettias, and flannel drapery in a show of old time ostentation.

When we got there it was dark. There was a sea of people spilling out onto the sidewalk and down the street in front of the hotel. My mother and father pushed into the back of the crowd and I followed after them maintaining a disinterested orbit, trying to ignore the holiday cheer.

The group moved forward, inch by inch. Small shuffling steps created a tidal pull that eventually drew us into the middle of the crowd. I was staring at my shoes and then out into the empty sidewalk on the opposite side of the street. I noticed that my parents had moved ahead of me. Three or four people separated us. They seemed to levitate in a little sphere of familiarity, awash in strange faces and foreign smells; all their bitter fighting and incongruities tucked into their wool jackets and forced public smiles.

A few minutes later, I looked up and saw that they were still further away. I was mulling in the crowded courtyard and they had been sucked up to the front entrance twenty feet away. The light of the hotel lobby was a loud yellow blare. I saw my dad turn around on the threshold. He grinned at me and nodded his chin. I could see the shadows in the pits of his eyes; the gray of his hair and the harsh lighting made his face look old and fragile.

He turned around and kept moving forward with my mother. After a few more minutes they were so far away that I could barely tell where they were. The backs of their heads were almost indistinguishable from any other couple in the sea of people. I felt terrible and alone.

Everything changes with time. Everything goes away. Sex is like a life jacket against that inevitable pull. Every new moment of sex with someone you love is a small victory of togetherness, a reminder that the other person is still there, for a while longer. Thinking about them out there, clinging to some other body, I wouldn't feel jealous. I think I would just feel terribly, horribly sad, reminded of the fact that one day they'll have gone out so far that they won't come back.

My First Muff Dive

The first woman I ever went down on had vagina boogers. Being my first time, I wasn't sure what to make of the green, pearly balls that were snaring in her pubic hair. I briefly thought that it might be what happens to a woman when she gets really turned on. Men ejaculate pearly goop and women shoot little boogers out of their vaginas. This thought was very soon overtaken by the realization that, whatever these gummy little pellets were, they had begun to taste an awful lot like balsamic vinegar and, whatever the state of my partner's arousal, that couldn't be a good sign. So then add vaginosis to the tally of strange things that I've eaten in my lifetime.

I love oral sex. It's a base level instinct I have; I want to taste my partner's vagina, in some way. Once the meet-and-greet formalities are out of the way and I realize I'm with someone I'd like to have sex with, I want to taste them. I don't think of this as a particularly macho convention. There's a tendency for men to become jocular about their skills at oral sex. It's another form of projecting dominance. I have no idea if I'm good at it or not, I just know I like it. There may, in fact, be a disconnect between liking it and being good at it. I sometimes find myself fixated on the textures and flavors and geography for long moments, marveling at the strange geography of someone else's body. Then I realize that ponderously running my tongue over the outer labia for a few minutes isn't getting my partner any further down the orgasm conveyor belt and I've got to spring back into more choreographed action.

Still, performing oral sex can be humiliating. It's like trying to write a novel in hieroglyphics. Our genitals are mysteries to one another. The schematics are simple enough, but, like driving a car with a manual transmission, there is a long distance between the owner's manual and the shifting of gears in heavy traffic. If I've doled out my fair share of lousy head, I can be comforted in the fact that most of the blowjobs I've had have been remarkably boring. Even the technically skilled ones that seemed to know what they were doing missed some fundamental point that seemed so obvious to me, having the added benefit of a direct understanding of my own body.

But this was no savior from the sourness I was drawing into my mouth, one tongue-lap at a time. I have since learned that any sexual act should be one of consideration and not just arousal. Conditions that might adversely affect your partners experience should, fairly, be advertised in advance. I'm sure I knew this at the time too, but there is often a gap between rhetorical principles you understand and those you're willing to act on. As I continued to coat my tongue and lips in acrid fluids, I began to suspect that the little coagulations might be a bad sign and not a good one.

This thought was followed by a feeling of sudden loneliness. As I searched for some inlet of ecstasy in between her legs, it seemed like I had fallen a few feet further away from the sweet face looking down at me from the headboard, as if an emulsion of despair had been squeezed out of my brain in the process of trying to understand what I was doing, and how it might be done to better effect. She was patiently watching me fail her. The absence of heavy breath or cambering moans made the silence feel like an inky mirror for my incompetence. And then her face changed. Her eyebrows lifted, pulling the ends of her smile upward with them. She put her hand on my shoulder and squeezed it softly. You don't have to waste your time anymore, she seemed to be saying. Come back to me, up here.

I pulled my naked body back up over hers and slowly kissed her, thinking I might regain her confidence and admiration in that slightly less mysterious act. I ran my hand from her hip back between her legs, some part of my brain still fixated on the strange mystery of failure. Perhaps my fingers could succeed where my mouth had failed. I traced a line upward with my index finger and then slid it inside her, trying to use the knob of bone where the finger met the palm of my hand as a hinge. I suspected there was some use to be had of my middle finger at this point and I tried to run it along the outer fold of skin while rocking my index finger back and forth. I was able to keep this up for only slightly longer than my first experiment with ice skating backward, only instead of falling my middle finger succumbed to symmetry and slipped into her vagina to redouble the movement of my index finger.

If this wasn't a fantastically effective act, it seemed to offer a respite from the falling hopelessness I'd experienced a few feet below. After another minute I choose to follow the security of mathematics and continue to add on to whatever it was that wasn't openly failing and so I slid my ring finger in, forming a thick bundle of digits. For a few seconds it seemed sustainable, and then I felt her head pull away from my craned, kissing face.

'Umm,' she said, 'I think three fingers is too many.'

Oh, of course. I quickly withdrew all of my fingers and searched my imagination for something else to do, but every spark of a thought extinguished itself in a gloom of ineffectual failure.

'Do you want to maybe put something inside me other than a finger?' she said.

'Oh, sure,' I said. Reverting to sex after having failed at every-thing else was an idea that never would have occurred to me. I had thought sex was something one arrived at after having successfully passed through all the preliminary topography of arousal, not a failsafe to fall back on when nothing else was working. Maybe this is what having sex is, I thought. I don't know.

I leaned over into the nightstand and found a condom in the drawer. I carefully tore open the glinting packet and carefully capped my penis with the thin rubber disk inside. I rolled it down with a strange muffling sensation, like trying to listen to someone through water-clogged ears. Then we had sex, and three minutes later I came.

Date With a Parking Ticket In It

I don't like daytime dates. Which is to say that I like them a lot with people I know. There's nothing happier than an afternoon spent in casual recline, chasing words and ideas around with someone familiar in an overcast bar or on a sunny stretch. It's easier to improvise in the daytime, and the improvisation more likely to be genuine when you know the person. Everything is open, everyone is out on the street, transportation is everywhere, opportunity looms. It's distracting to spend those hours in a verbal slow dance with a stranger from the internet. Still, I agreed to meet G for coffee one Saturday afternoon.

I woke up late. I had slept nine hours the night before but I was still sluggish from the kind of heavy sleep that comes after a week of four and five hour nights. I felt achy and confused. I had an hour to take the slouching mantis with bedhair and turn him into a suave and engaged human being.

And then it was suddenly five minutes after we were supposed to have met and I hadn't even left my apartment. I grabbed my jacket and texted G an excuse about stopping by the bank on the way over. I showed up twenty minutes late. G was waiting for me at a table outside. It was cold and cloudy and the coffee shop was overstuffed with people. I thought I was really testing my limits showing up twenty minutes late. Women aren't supposed to be kept waiting for their men, especially on a first date. I expected her to be fuming and passive aggressive.

But G didn't seem upset when I arrived. She had ordered me a coffee, but had left the cup unfilled so it wouldn't get cold before I got there. I was briefly touched. I'm pretty sure I wouldn't have bothered ordering something for someone else in advance on a first date. G was pretty and tall, thought it was hard to really see how tall she was because she was sitting down and her length was obscured by her angular posture and a floppy angora sweater.

I have no idea what we talked about during those first few minutes. It was cold and my brain was still running slowly. I was preoccupied with work and was overcompensating by trying to get her to talk about her work so I wouldn't have to think and speak at the same time. I became aware that I was clinching my body down into a ball to preserve body heat against the cold afternoon air. G mentioned another coffee shop that was nearby, which would at least get us out of the cold. She had driven into the San Francisco from Oakland and we walked to her car so she could drive us to the next spot. It was a ten-minute walk from where we were but she seemed intent on driving.

When I lived in Los Angeles I drove my Dad's 1994 Geo Metro with 320,000 miles on the engine. It was old and insulated with all sorts of detritus that my dad had accumulated over the years. Random receipts, air fresheners, a glove, bungee cords, a folded up tarp, multiple flashlights. Seeing G's car made me think of what the women I used to take out in the Metro must have thought getting into the passenger seat while I held the door open. Her car was a weather worn sedan from the 80's that had a clatter of stuff on every surface. It was the kind of car that always has something in the passenger seat that needs to be cleared off before someone can get in.

As we went into the next coffee shop I tried to peek at G's figure. She moved like a giraffe, with wide hips and a flat butt. She was almost as tall as I was. I started to imagine all the things I could do with a pair of long legs during sex. Then I noticed she was wearing boots and began to worry about what her feet would look like. Then we were ordering coffee and settling into a new table before I could carry myself away with foot thoughts.

We spent another few minutes talking. She started telling me a story about growing up on a farm and how she had helped name her family's horses. I started to get the one-hour itch. I was tired of hearing stories. I liked her. I was attracted to her. I started to steal glances at her lips and the freckles on her sternum behind her scarf and loosening sweater collar. I didn't want to listen, I wanted to kiss. It was like I was at a car dealership. The salesman had sold me on the feature list and now I wanted to stop looking at the pamphlet and drive.

People aren't cars, I realize. I didn't like G well enough to commit to the same kind of relationship that I might have made with a car at a dealership. I'd begun mistrusting these impulses to escalate first dates according to my bored whims of romance. There's an element of cruelness in deciding that you like someone enough to kiss them but not enough to listen to them. 'Behave,' I told myself. 'Pretend like you're a grownup man capable of taking someone else's thoughts and experiences more seriously than the ego rush of random public stroking.'

So I listened to more of G's stories. I tried to tell some of my own, my history with horses, the unexpected labors of maintaining a healthy garden, the stupidity of wine snobbery. It was less fun than kissing, even if it made me feel like a slightly more responsible person. It wasn't bad, it was delayed gratification. We talked about tangoing and made vague plans to go dancing together after the holidays. The idea seemed nice. The length of time between a mid-December coffee and some nebulous tango date 'after the holidays' was comforting.

When we left, G found out that she had gotten a parking ticket. I felt a brief impulse to split it with her, though I'm pretty sure there is no social convention that dictates anything about tickets and dates. 'That sucks,' I said. I couldn't figure out if it was a bad omen that she had gotten a ticket, or a good sign that she had been so interested in our conversation that she had forgotten to check on the parking meter. I didn't know if I cared one way or the other.

We should have met at night, I am thought as I walked home, in some dark corner of a bar and we should have kissed until it became indecent. We have the whole rest of our lives to be mature, to discuss our childhoods and social grudges. What does that have to do with a date?

Two Women in One Night

There are a lot of things I've never done in my life. Picking up two women in one night is on that list, though now I can cross it off. For whatever it's worth. When I was 13 I used to tell my friends that I was a honey magnet. I couldn't look a girl in the eye for longer than a few seconds, much less serve as some kind of magnet to which honeys would gravitate in some kind of knee-buckling frenzy. I had a mullet at the time and as far as I understand mullets are the diametric opposite of magnets.

I didn't fare much better as I grew older. I was a serious boy with serious designs on becoming a poet, a composer, a philanthropist; I wanted to transform myself into some austere lover from a Michael Ondaatje novel. This persona went over about as well as a mullet at college parties and the bars I skulked through in my early 20s. It's a nice prize of aging that you can take yourself less and less seriously the further away from these youthful identity delusions one gets.

When I passed thirty I managed to lose that fictive chip on my shoulder. I began to provide for myself all that serious intimacy that I so needfully sought in other people as an angry 15-year-old. Instead, I began to want only someone who'd tolerate my dirty jokes and want to lick me without prompting. Which is to say that I don't have expectations of people anymore. Combining that with the emotional distance I began keeping with other women after N left made me a much more appealing to women than I'd ever been.

To wit, I went to Dolores Park one night to meet a woman for a bottle of wine and, with luck, some cigarettes. Whether or not the company turned out to be amusing, I was going to have a pleasant night getting drunk on the grass with the San Francisco skyline blinking on in slow motion as the sun dropped behind the western fog.

I showed up early to find a nice spot with a good view, uncorked the wine, and then H arrived. I was attracted to H as soon as I saw her. She had a pretty face, an ebullient smile, and seemed like one of those special people who is permanently tanned. We had boring conversation about work, the past, and all the regular checklist subjects. I laughed lots to cover up my boredom. I think we had been together for 45 minutes before I got sick of talking. I looked away from her for a few seconds to create a pause in the conversation. It worked. She took a breath and looked out at the skyline. I turned back and stared at her face in profile, wondering what her mouth would taste like. I leaned in so she wouldn't start talking again. She saw me coming and turned into me and we kissed. It was soft and nice. I pulled back to catch her eye for a moment, then kissed her again, working the tip of my tongue just inside the rim of her upper lip.

After a few minutes I sat back. 'Now's my chance to get a cigarette,' I thought. I asked if she smoked as nonchalantly as possible, and soon we were huffing away on her menthol 100s. The sun was almost down and shimmered in the glass of the downtown skyscrapers. There was a soft Indian summer breeze. I was on my second glass of wine, the hint of someone else's saliva on my lips. Things were nice.

We spent the next couple of hours kissing in the park, hardly talking at all. It was fun, like playing a pickup game of basketball in a schoolyard with some strangers – improvisatory and distantly athletic and surrounded by relative anonymity. I have no idea what makes me attractive to women. I have no concept of what I must look like through their eyes during a conversation or at close range. H was nice enough, but I had little interest in her. I laughed when she told funny stories, but I didn't go out of my way to offer my own. I sat by passively, smiling here and there, quipping along just enough, but I was unengaged. I was a counterweight to the conversation, but I wasn't ever present in it.

We both had outs for later in the evening, though we tarried until 11 or so, when we finally retreated to our separate corners. I went out for another drink with a friend afterwards. We wound up in a quiet bar and had a man-talk about women, work, politics, and commuting. Then another woman, a sparky brunette with short hair and profligate freckles, came up to me with some line about a bet she'd made with her friends about my occupation. She'd guessed I was a furniture designer. She was cocky and well-rehearsed and seemed tantalizingly disappointed when I told her I was a writer.

We thrusted and parried for a few more minutes and then she retreated to her waiting friends. Before going home I ambled over to her table and we exchanged numbers. I cared very little about meeting women at that moment, for once in my life. True to form, that was when I'd suddenly become most attractive to them. I'm sure there are people out there for whom hooking up with one person in the evening and then being picked up on by another person is de rigueur. For me it's absurd. It's a delightful ego stroke, and absurdly fun to experience. But it's about as gratifying as the aisle of Twinkies in the 7-Eleven.

And still, my inner 13-year-old gloated like a stuffed pig.

H's Version of Our Night Out

Soon after I wrote about her, H discovered the story. I think it's fair to say she was unhappy with what I had written. I asked H if she would be willing to share what her experience of our time together. I'd taken described my selfish memory of our time together but was eager to join that distant gloating with its inextricable counterpart. She accepted the offer and what follows is her recounting of our date. My only preemptory comment will be this: I was born in Kenya. I am not South African, nor have I ever been to South Africa.

Now H's story:

'As I walk into Dolores Park to meet South Africa man, he sends a text to let me know he's wearing a purple shirt and is sitting beneath a baby palm tree. Purple shirt guy might be boring, might be rude, might need intensive therapy, might be gorgeous, and might be fun. Half expecting that he'll be awful; I'm stoked that cocktails will be involved. He promised to bring wine. I have plans afterward with a girlfriend, so either way I'll have a fun evening. I'm new to San Francisco, and making new friends is far more important to me than finding myself involved in a romantic relationship. That said, I'm completely emotionally available and am open to meeting someone extraordinary, otherwise I wouldn't even be here.

I round the palm and see him. He's beautiful, but I decide that I am more beautiful and I find comfort in knowing that I have an edge here in the balance of power. Beautiful South Africa man stands and we exchange a hug and kiss. He pours wine into two animal print coffee cups. I choose the cheetah print and he teases me about being a fast girl. He's casually dressed in cute jeans, a faded purple shirt that says 'Hang Loose', striped blue socks and bright lemon-colored shoes. It sounds like a bad combination, but he completely pulls off the look and I like it. I compliment his shoes. 'They are yellow,' he says. 'I know my colors,' I say. He comments that he likes mine as well. Unless he paid close attention while I slipped them off, I know he cannot see them. My shoes are behind me and out of his view. I ask him what kind of shoes I am wearing. He laughs and owns up to not knowing.

He shares his hatred for feet and we both agree that it's weird that his coworkers tend to walk around at the office in white tube socks. He asks me a work question and then apologizes immediately. He hates talking about work. Perfect, because so do I. 'Tell me a story,' he says. I share a story that I had just discussed that morning involving a girlfriend's bombed Valentine's Day earlier this year. Her boyfriend broke up with her on Valentine's Day. Fabulous girl that she is, she put on her sexy new lingerie, and drank an excessive amount of champagne while feasting on the crab and oysters that she had planned to share with the boyfriend. While cracking open one of the oyster shells, the knife slipped and she had to be taken to the hospital in her lingerie for stitches in her hand and wrist, which without explanation appeared to be a suicide attempt. Beautiful South Africa guy shares that he's never had a great Valentine's Day. He asks if I have and I just say 'yes.' Sharing a hot Valentine's Day story about a previous boyfriend doesn't seem appropriate ten minutes into a first date.

He leans in and kisses me. It's perfect. It's soft and sweet. He pulls away and shares that he 'just wanted to try it out.' He leans in again and we kiss for a few more minutes. I love kissing and we kiss well together. I'm also aware that we are in a public park and try my best to fight back a bit of laughter. I usually require a bit more alcohol to engage in PDA with a stranger. While I wasn't necessarily ready to kiss South Africa, I completely indulge myself in a fabulous make-out session. He shares that he's been in the city for almost a year and we banter about how he could spend his little anniversary with the city. I suggest the Kabuki Spa having just been for the first time after a day of surfing. It's such a relaxing and lovely way to spend an afternoon or evening with oneself.

He asks me if I smoke. I do. He asks if I mind giving him a cigarette. We've been drinking wine for about an hour and I was just planning on having one myself. We spend the next few hours kissing in the park. The sun is setting and we have a gorgeous view of the city. I realize that I don't really know anything more about South Africa than I knew before walking into the park. I know that he dislikes co-workers cruising around the office in their socks. I know that he was born in Africa, but not South Africa. I forget where exactly but still continue to refer to him as South Africa merely because I like how it sounds. I know that he buys striped socks. I know that he has amazing hair which feels incredibly hot to run my fingers through. I know his name and I know that he is an amazing kisser. For a first date, that's good enough for me.

We both have plans later in the evening. I'm meeting a girlfriend for drinks around 10 and he has a friend coming over around 9.30. He invites me over to meet his man friend and for us to have a cocktail before we each go out. I agree. Nothing says serial killer or sexual sadist about beautiful South Africa man. Maybe it's his expensive and fashionable glasses or his bright yellow shoes. We walk hand-in-hand and intermittently stop to kiss along the way and in the elevator on our way up to his apartment. Beautiful South Africa's man friend is fantastic, and mixes all sorts of random and delicious drinks for us. I'm certain to have a hangover.

Man friend asks whether I have seen South Africa's photographs from when he was in the Peace Corps. I have not. He insists that I see them. Did I know that beautiful South Africa man is making a film and is the director? Have I seen his fantastic pair of pink shoes? It's all so cute. Man friend is trying to make beautiful South Africa seem very cool for what I perceive to be my benefit. I ask for a few embarrassing stories, he doesn't give any up. He's a loyal man friend. After viewing the Peace Corps photos, I realize that beautiful South Africa has only recently grown into his adult hotness. He's 'new hot' and I find that attractive. I've never been a huge fan of guys who know they are good looking. The knowing of one's hotness generally corresponds with a certain level of arrogance that I find unattractive. I step out to the terrace and call Tara who is lounging around in her panties and her bra and who is now contemplating staying in. I hadn't realized the time and am late to meet her. She needs a few minutes to pull it together so I have a few more sips of man friend's drink concoctions.

Beautiful South Africa is attentive and affectionate with me in front of his man friend. He holds my hand, kisses me and wraps his arms around me intermittently while we chat and share drinks. I excuse myself to use the bathroom and return to find beautiful South Africa and man friend setting up Wii Golf. Do I want to play? Man friend hands me a remote and I decide it is time to go for sure. I feel like something shifted in the mood. Man friend is visiting from out of town, my girlfriend is waiting for me and I think video games are silly. When I share that I am leaving, I find it funny when beautiful South Africa man asks if it's because they are playing videogames. Funny 'ish' because I slightly feel that he is gauging whether setting up video games is a sure way to get a girl to leave one's apartment. Given his behavior throughout the evening, I hadn't considered that he might actually want me to leave.

He offers to walk with me to my girlfriend Tara's apartment, which is a few blocks away. We walk hand in hand. When we arrive, he shares that he will be busy filming all next week and weekend, but that he would like to see me again the week afterward. He also suggests that I call him earlier if I'm available. I'm not a 'call first kind of girl' and explain that while I'd love to see him again, he should call me. He calls me old fashioned before we share an amazing kiss goodbye. I climb the stairs to

Tara's apartment with a huge smile on my face and am excited to share all the details of my date.

I'm a complete girly girl and gush over my date's gorgeous hair, that I think his glasses are sexy, how well we kiss together, and how he's easy to talk to. I again realize that I don't really know anything more about him, but don't really care. I assume that I'll see him again. Tara throws on a gorgeous new dress and we walk to a nearby bar. We have an entertaining conversation about beautiful South Africa man, her new love interest, dating in general, and then of course go back to her apartment and have a pillow fight in our bra and panties. The week passes and I'm secretly a little bummed that beautiful South Africa man hasn't called. I never considered that he wasn't interested in seeing me again. Not because I'm arrogant, but because of the level of affection he showed throughout our date. I generally think I'm a good judge of a man's interest in me. The confidence in this skill has recently disappeared.

The following Sunday, I find myself leisurely playing online and decide to check out the Nerve magazine site which is generally entertaining enough. I see beautiful South Africa man's photo alongside other photos and various articles. I assume that he must have upgraded his membership and has a highlighted profile. I skim various articles and come to a catchy article title about two women in the same night written by some guy who once sported a mullet. It takes me a few paragraphs to realize that I am reading an article written by beautiful South Africa man about our date. I have been reviewed and it's not good.

I call Tara. I call Katie. I call Rachel. I read the key phrases in the article to each of them, which note that he thought I was 'boring,' how he kissed me so that I 'wouldn't start talking again,' how he 'laughed lots to cover up his boredom,' and that he had 'little interest' in me. I'm both injured and amused. He's really not into me? I have a fairly healthy ego and I decide it will be funny to print the article and put it on my refrigerator. I own a copy of He's Just Not That into You. My friends and I don't need this book to guide our love lives. We think it's ridiculous that women need someone to point out that if a man is not calling you, or is married, or is not having sex with you, then he's probably not interested. There is not however a chapter cautioning women that a man may not being interested in you if he spends the evening kissing you, holding your hand, laughing attentively while you share stories and inviting you to his apartment to meet one of his friends followed up by a decoded man version explanation that kissing may be his way of quieting you and that his laughter covers boredom.

While this is the first time to my knowledge that anyone has ever called me boring, I obsess over the next few days. I overanalyze my fun level and charm and am annoyed that a few paragraphs written by a man I hardly know have had such an effect on me. Dating can absolutely suck. It can be expensive, disappointing and a humbling experience. It can also be wildly romantic and allow ourselves to explore new interests and places with amazing new people. After a few days, I finally stop obsessing and I realize that we are all reviewed by the people we encounter in our lives. And in the end, the only reviews that really matter are the ones we give ourselves. Beautiful South Africa man does not need to think I am fun nor interesting because I think I am just fabulous!'

Are You My Girlfriend Now?

I once dated a woman for five months and, without any prompting, started to think of her as my girlfriend. I wasn't seeing anyone else, and we spent a lot of time together. By the third month we would talk almost daily. Texts were exchanged throughout the day, evenings were spent eating together or cocooned on a couch watching television.

I wondered whether we had crossed some formal threshold without realizing it. I remember sitting on her couch one night watching television, a show I would have found tedious under any other circumstance, but seeing it with her gave it a new bearable quality. 'This is what I would be doing with my girlfriend on a Tuesday night,' I thought to myself. 'So are you my girlfriend now?'

The more I thought about the question, the less I cared about the answer. I wasn't seeing anybody else and I didn't feel the need to look any further. I felt content. I had someone to laugh with, someone to eat and drink with, and someone to curl up beside on the couch at the end of a stupid Tuesday night. I didn't care if she was seeing anyone else. It didn't seem like it, she never flaked on me or had excuses spilling out of her purse at inopportune moments.

Things were comfortable and convenient. It was so easy that I thought it might be better if she were seeing other people. It might have made things seem like less of a concession. Getting together with someone because it's easy is not good news. The longer we went without confronting that piece of taxonomical housekeeping, the easier it would be for me to leave when the comfort became too much. Three months later I was seeing someone else.

I asked N to be my girlfriend two weeks after we'd started seeing each other. Actually, I asked her if she'd be my girlfriend 'for six weeks.' I had known when we were introduced that she was moving to New York. That fact was still abstract and unfixed. I'd only just met her, and still the finish line was set hard and fast up ahead. I didn't ask her to be my girlfriend because I wanted to know what she would say. It wasn't a question. I knew what we were together.

In the space of a few weeks she had become a bright new center of gravity for me. She was inevitable. When I got her texts at work they didn't feel like surprising reminders that she existed. Instead they appeared like a wave that has finally reached the shore after having been watched, slowly building out at sea.

When I asked her, it was a declaration, not a question. It was a confession. I want you to be my girlfriend.

It's an arbitrary label to apply to someone, and it doesn't really change what's between two people. A label doesn't add intimacy or security, it just alleviates the stress of worrying about what comes next.

'Yes, I'll be your girlfriend for six weeks,' she said, smiling in the dim bar light. It didn't change anything. It felt good to give an outward showing of how strong my feelings were. It was nice to see her smile because of it. That was all I meant.

She left six weeks later. All I had left was a stupid placard with some old title on it, oxidizing with each passing minute.

Natasha Richardson, or Smoking Cigarettes on the Roof

The first thing I heard on my alarm radio one morning was that Natasha Richardson had died of complications from a skiing accident. I had been asleep for five hours and it was still dark outside when the blare of the radio announcer reported her death. From that morose news he seamlessly transitioned into The Supremes.

I've never been in love with someone who died. The first dead body I saw was my grandmother's. She died in a small mobile home near my parents' house. Before the people from the hospital came to pick her up my dad asked me to come down and see her one last time. I had been with her two days earlier, when she was still alive. She was tired and in pain. She had a stress fracture in her spine and was in constant pain because of it.

I was scared walking into the bedroom of her flimsy little shack. The walls were thin and I could feel the floor bending underneath me. I was filled with superstition. A mobile of ghoulish imagery rotated around my mind: wrinkled and dangling flesh, toothless mouths, animalistic grunting. I was afraid my frail little grandmother, who stopped and pointed every time she saw a bird and made farting noises when she got up after dinner, had turned into some gnarled distortion of her former self. I was afraid that, in death, she would have trans-formed into a monster.

Instead, she was just empty. Her face was neutral and quiet. Her body was lying flat along the plastic lined twin bed that she slept on. My father had folded her arms across her chest and put a few small flowers in her hand. She was the same as she had been, just a little bit colder and stiller. She was gone, but she was still there in almost every way that I had come to recognize her by.

A week before N left San Francisco we spent half the weekend together. We'd gone out drinking on Friday night and stayed up late. We woke up again sometime in the afternoon on Saturday, had sex, slept, had sex again, and then she became aware of all the things still left to pack that surrounded us. The sun was starting to go down and the evening wind was gusting. We were suppose to go out separately that night. She had a going-away party with some friends I didn't know and I had promised my boss I would come to his housewarming party.

I remember lying next to her in bed, the daylight slowly graying and losing heat around us. I felt her warm, naked body against the length of my own body; a little envelope of heat where they met. Her head lay in the crook of my arm and when I looked at her face the first thing I could see was the curly line of small hairs running in an wild arc across her forehead. Her apartment was lined with stacks of half-filled moving boxes. We were drinking frozen sake from red plastic cups.

We went up onto the roof of her building to smoke. I put on one of her sheer silk robes, spilling over with paisley, a gift from her mother that she never wore. We sat against the waist-high ledge that guarded the front of the building, looking south on the city. Everything was white and twinkling in the heatless light. The wind felt cold and kept blowing our robes open.

I put my arm around her and pulled her against me. I was shivering a little from the cold and the slushy sake. I teased her about something. She smiled and leaned in closer to me, pressing her arms up to her chest to hold in the heat. I felt like a ghost and an angel. Something inside me had switched over, a small floodgate was gushing out happiness. There was no urgency, everything was serene and far away, a composed miniature. It was cold, but the coldness kept pushing me closer to her.

And then we pulled apart.

Ass Bangin' and Astral Projection

I can't remember exactly how old I was the first time I put a finger into my own ass, but I remember liking it. I was probably 15 or 16. I was so guilt ridden about it after the fact that I walked around the house for hours torturing myself with the idea that I was probably gay. What other implication could there be for a man to inserting something into his ass? It's difficult to escape the power play implications with anything involving a man's behind. Putting something into someone else's ass is macho; putting something into your own hindquarters is a lilting defeat. The alpha and the limp-wristed beta.

It's the same idea that underscores thinking about dick size and the entirety of sexual expression in a culture where sex is a commoditized lever to manipulate people's insecurities. Sex is a blunt instrument that you exercise, correctly or incorrectly, on your supine partner whose receipt of your unbridled sex thrust is an acknowledgement of his or her powerlessness before the mighty cock.

Stripped of all its macho connotations, though, the ass is just another collection of nerve endings that can be used to pleasure yourself or your partner. The presence of the prostate lying dormant a few inches inside is a double win for men ready to loosen up their instinctive recoil against letting themselves become the receiver for one mortifying moment.

Ass play is a kind of sexual dissociative. The sensory experience of sex for a man is typically wound up in the act of penetrating, and the specific group of sensations that come along with it. Feeling yourself penetrated at the same time that you are enjoying the metaphysical whoosh of penetrating someone else is surreal. It's an out of body experience, like an alien abduction or astral projection. It's like being in two separate places at once, wholly conscious of everything around you.

One of the enduring mysteries of heterosexual sex is the distinction between penis and vagina. No matter how much rhetorical information we might pick up in afterglow confessions or coffee shop dishing, men will never really understand what it feels like to have a vagina nor will women ever understand the sensation of having a penis. I used to lament this fact when I was younger. Talking to some of my girlfriends about their orgasms I felt jealous that a hummer and gradual build up to ejaculation would be my only sexual prizes. It's nice but when there's talk of 20 minutes of roiling orgasm where the whole world turns a different color, it's hard not think of getting one's nut off as a milky consolation prize.

Is ass play the key to breaking into this orgasmic ether? There's something undeniably complete about uniting the act of penetrating and being penetrated in one person. It also seems to be a pleasure that's unique to the male libido. What's the female analog for penetrating?

Ass play can certainly be a complicated; it often requires a good deal more attention to timing, logistics, and manners than most other sex acts. But in the end it's just another fundament in the language of sex. Avoiding it is sort of like dating someone who insists that you never bring up politics or religion with them. It's not like politics or religion are so inherently important to a relationship, but the focus on them as immutable taboos are surely an indicator of some basic dysfunction. Likewise, fixating on 'banging' someone's ass is like filibustering a conversation. An empty bit of formalism that gives the appearance of function but whose primary purpose is to prevent progress and avoid confrontation with the other side.

I Was a Six-Year-Old Virgin

When I was growing up I believed in the idea of being a virgin until marriage. My parents were religious and I had to go to church with them every week, but my reasoning didn't have anything to do with god. I came home after school one day when I was six or seven and watched an episode of The Phil Donahue Show, in which the subject was people who were saving their first sexual experiences for marriage. One of the panelists was wearing a white wedding gown, and while I don't remember anything that was said on the show, I felt swept away by the idea. It was like I had suddenly been given the words to articulate a romantic impulse that had been welling up in my little adolescent body.

The idea that two people could be predestined for each other, so connected that they should preserve their most intimate selves until the day when they could finally commit to one another was revelatory. My friend C told me, with eyes rolling, that I'm in love with my own ability to be in love. Watching Donahue as a wide-eyed kid I felt like there was a missing half for me, going about her life unaware of my existence. It was my task to find her, and preserving my virginity as some hairless expression of my faith that we would be together became an imperative.

It's good to be six years old.

As an adult, the idea is silly. How could love be a force for holding you back from experiencing new things? Of the women I have been in love with, I can't imagine wanting any of them to forgo an experience simply out of deference to me. This is an image of love as a yoke, a weight of obligation slung around your partner's neck, constricting them with your need for emotional constancy. It's easy to fixate on the process of finding love, the simple nursery rhyme of discovery. The real feat of falling in love is figuring out how to live with it for a lifetime after you've stumbled across it in a bar, a classroom, or a friend's party.

I have no idea what I want. I want constancy and comfort in the same way I want to eat the whole pint of ice cream in one sitting. It's perfectly logical until the instinct has been sated and there's nothing left but wallowing and bloat, the dizzy afterglow of having gorged on something rich, sweet, and lacking any sustaining qualities. I don't know if I can be in a long-term relationship. The 6-year-old controlling the knobs and levers of my heart wants it.

How can you stay together with someone for a long period of time, lives intrinsically connected, and not become a burden to one another? Having watched my parents fight and torture each other while I was growing up, it's tempting to imagine they both would have been more content and fulfilled living separately. Love eventually transforms from melodic idealism into a pragmatic riddle. The charm, wit, and closeness become repetition and predictability, while new wrinkles and morning breath to make the fading luster seem even more indignant.

I don't know if that's true, but it's what I fear. When I was six the idea of promising away the whole of my life seemed like an imperative. Now that I've seen all the ways I've changed up until this point, it's a scary idea to think about promising someone I'll still be with them when I'm 60. Especially when there's a 6-year-old in control of that part of my heart.

Morning Breath

I've always been self-conscious about my breath. I grew up with an older brother who made sport of trapping me in clouds of reek that came from his various orifices. I have acute memories of the fetid air that came out of his mouth in the mornings. As a pissed-off teenager it was easy to come to the conclusion that my brother's breath smelled that way simply as a reflection of what a horrible person he was: loud, obnoxious, prone to tyrannical outbursts of violence. How could his breath not smell like a dying possum in a sewer?

This was the first time I ever considered the fact that I also might have bad breath in the morning. I didn't just consider it, I took as an irrevocable fact. I could never really get a sense for the state of my breath, whether it was rancorous or neutral, but the memory of my brother's breath from my childhood always left me suspicious that common genes left me susceptible to all his physiological shortcomings.

This is an unfortunate because I am fond of morning kissing. Waking up with someone, seeing their face inches from yours, the first light of day swelling at the blinds, it's hard to think of something to do other than kiss. Life is too short, filled with obstacles and reasons things fail or fall apart. Waking up close to someone I care about, I've always felt a dopey sense of luck. It makes my body want to speak, and the most instinctive language is a kind of a kiss.

The great cosmic joke is that, in this happy bath of felicitude, there's eight hours of digestive exhaust and stale bedroom air hovering in between. Touching lips for the first time in the morning – still in bed, no time yet for toothbrushing or gargling – is a kind of blunt physical intimacy. It's a test, to see if your love and attraction can endure the physical realities of your partner's most unromanticized form. I look like a bleary-eyed pile of trash in the morning. Even after a full night my face goes pale, my wrinkle lines deepen, and my hair turns into an entropic molding. Add in a night of boozing and cigarettes and it's almost too much to think about what fallibly pungent vessel it is that you're foisting on her.

I remember some mornings with N, the first touch of our dry lips, nudging them open softly, breaking the shy seal of morning mouth, the first warm breath mixing together, dank and fecund, slowly rubbing the wetness from the inner lip outward. The first shy probe of the tongue, not wanting to overwhelm the other person, slowly widening until the whole mouth is open, sexual, past waking.

I noticed over time that she had the distinct taste of broccoli in the morning. I remember recognizing the taste for the first time, and quietly marveling at the fact that I actually liked it. If this were my brother, or some one-night stand, it might have been overwhelming. With N it was sweet, another part of her that I wanted to touch and hold (or lick, as it were). I came to crave it, even while I knew the idea might once have been nauseatingly inconceivable.

Premature Ejaculation

When I was in high school I imagined that being able to hold out for more than three or four minutes during sex was a rite of passage. Watching porno and listening to other men talk about their sexual experiences I figured it was something that just inevitably happened, like baldness. I was wrong.

I always experience a moment of doubt when I'm sleeping with someone new and we're about to have sex for the first time. It's hard not to get carried away on the wave of excitement and physical discovery, which is usually when I start to wonder whether or not my sprinkler head is going to go off too soon after entry. There are few things quite as soul crushing as feeling like you've got to apologize for something after sex.

I have a decent understanding of the varying levels and intensities of my own arousal and what it means for my prospects of coming. With a little extra management and thought it's easy enough to keep everything at a maintainable level of without getting the sneezy tingles. Still, there are times when it all evaporates with a vague momentum that suddenly rematerializes in a few irreversible seconds of spasm.

It's nice to think that lovemaking can be reduced to a handful of colloquial rules of thumb, but sex always surprises me. I can't think of a single experience I've had where there wasn't something new or unexpected. I'm surprised enough by all the subtle shifts and new aspects of my own body: a fleshy callous felt from the underside, the tangle of my hair in the mornings (which appears as a new form of mess almost every day), the veins of my forearm. The more you get to know something, the more it changes.

Having sex with someone new is a flood of new detail. Feeling the touch of a new hand, the taste of a new mouth, the sweat of skin, a new rhythm, new contours; there's so much happening all at once that keeping track of my own arousal slips a few notches in importance. Then the moment is irrevocably at hand.

Other times, I come too soon because I just don't care about lasting longer. I get infatuated with my own immediate feelings and don't want to moderate them. I want the galloping rush to carry me in as far as it can. This is usually the least satisfying kind of sex. In the moment it seems like a great idea; the impulse to keep pushing faster and father is totally logical. Then the logic departs in anti-climax, the starry chariot that seemed to be ascending heavenward minutes earlier is transformed into a sweaty hulk with only a distant echo of thrill left inside.

I suspect this kind of low-level joy, the natural equivalent of popping a whip-it, is what makes it so easy for men to celebrate sex as something worth bragging about. This kind of sex is the ego running unrestrained, the dog off the leash bounding through the park with no understanding of where it's going or why.

For how much anxiety I've experienced over coming too soon, I've never gotten any real flack for it from the women I've been with. 'Don't let it get to your head,' N told me the first time we had sex for a good three minutes.

There's something private about having an orgasm. It can be like a little departure, watching your partner leave her body for a moment, eyes closed, moving in a silent rhythm of her own making. In the best cases, both people can go along to the same relative height, like looking at someone on opposite sides of an elevated chasm. Coming early is like being on a pretty mountaintop and not seeing anyone else, it's pretty and lonely, narcissistic and irresistible.

Having Sex at Weddings

It took a long time for some of my closer friends to start getting married. I was actually concerned, for a time, that I was being short-changed out of some boisterous life experience because no one I knew seemed capable of pledging away the rest of their lives in a public ceremony. If the universe rewards bravery then it also celebrates patience. The last several years have seen an outbreak of nuptial pageantry among my friends, and I have happily become the guest permanently circulating in the background, sipping white wine and flirting with tipsy aunts over cake.

One such wedding was in St. Louis. I was looking around the reception hall when my friend P pointed out two women standing on the edge of the dance floor holding their purses. 'Look, they're in estrus,' he said. It makes sense that people should feel more susceptible to romantic dalliances with all the reverberations of vows, speeches and an open bar hanging in the periphery. There's also the subconscious feeling that everyone present has been vouchsafed as a worthwhile human being through association. You don't need the same defensive barriers that you might normally employ at a bar when attending a wedding. The chances the nice young man in the fitted suit trying to start a conversation is secretly a creep seem lower. On the off chance that he is a creep, he's probably from out of town anyway, so let the hounds of love fly.

There's also a male equivalent of being in estrus at a wedding. If the flowers, dancing, and free range children spilling flower petals everywhere go straight to some women's brains, those same vaguely optimistic cues trigger a metaphysical change in men too. And there is the sense of opportunity, an instinctual foreknowledge that settles in as you enter a room full of drunken women wearing their best dresses and dancing to Justin

Timberlake. Hooking up with someone in that atmosphere, stranger or not, seems as natural as offering a handshake to someone's long lost uncle over a tray of appetizers.

Later that night I was dancing in a middle-aged bramble, trying not to slosh wine on the 3-year-olds that seemed to be sprouting like mushrooms on the dance floor. I saw the same two women that P had said were in estrus. They were standing against the wall talking to each other with well-heeled posture and attentive expressions. I felt the tickle of inevitability as I looked at the brunette. 'This will be the one I wind up sleeping with later,' I thought while two-stepping to Nelly.

I walked over, said hello, was joined by more friends, spent an hour in idle chatter, danced some more, and soon we were peeling away in clumps to head back downtown while the busboys shoo'd us out of the reception hall. We went to another bar, drank more, wound up alone against a far corner and started kissing. Kissing someone for the first time, drunk, and knowing you'll never see them again, is dislocating. I wasn't listening to her body at all. I wasn't paying attention to what her mouth was saying, I pressed with mine, looking for what I wanted, licking, biting, circling, pulling.

A few hours later when we were in bed it was the same thing. I had the vague sense that I was trying to breakdance on a floor with too much traction. I knew exactly what I wanted, but the more animated we became the farther away it got. Three hours later she sprung out of bed, showered, packed her bag, and disappeared in a taxi to the airport. I still couldn't pronounce her name right. We had sex all night long and I didn't come once. We went through an encyclopedia of positions and bounced off the bed twice. It was fun and about as satisfying as dancing in front of the mirror in my underpants while getting dressed in the morning.

At the breakfast brunch, nursing a hangover and wondering if anyone else noticed that I smelled like drunken sex, I watched the married couple listen to each other as they spoke to their relatives, completing each others thoughts, eating from the same plate. I felt like an albino wino. The open bar was closed, the flowers had been swept from the dance floor, the dry-cleaned formalwear had become wrinkled jeans and stubby tennis shoes, and strategically placed candlelight had become blaring, lonely, inconsolable daylight.

Intimacy on a Trip to the Dentist

I went to a new dentist a month after I moved to San Francisco. There are few things less pleasant than a rude thirty minutes spent in a dentist's chair having someone scrape at your teeth with a wiry metal instrument. But there is also a secret pleasure in going to the dentist; one that I can remember enjoying from my earliest visits as a boy. It's the experience of seeing someone else's face at such a close distance, hovering over mine. It's hard not to be drawn in by the chance to stare into someone's eyes just a few inches away with little or no understanding of who they are outside of the most basic professional identity.

I remember consciously choosing a female dentist when I had the list of providers from the insurance company open in front of me. I didn't even consider male dentists as I went down the column of names. Why? What was I expecting? I don't have any specific fetish for dental tools or the general aesthetics of medical offices. I don't think I was expecting to hit on my dentist or use oral hygiene as a pretext for an illicit affair with someone in a surgical mask and lab coat.

My dentist is a particularly neurotic sort of woman. Single, close to forty, painfully aware of the solitary little comma that separates those two facts, but still indifferent and self-possessed at the end of the sentence. Her pale freckled face floated over mine as she examined my gums. She propped my lips open with a rubber-gloved hand and rambled about salsa lessons she kept meaning to take, crazy ex-boyfriends that just couldn't commit, her dysfunctional family. I felt like I should answer back, like I was missing my turn in the conversational merry-go-round by not validating her experiences with agreeable one-liners.

With a mouth full of fingers, metal, and a suction tube to keep me from drooling, the best I could manage were primal grunts. I wound up staring and listening to the babbling stream of thoughts dribble down onto my face. Is there a suction tube in some alternate universe that patients could hold in dentists' mouths to keep them from going on too long about the price of apartments in Nob Hill or how they think everyone should live in New York once in their life (though it will never be the same as it was back then, in the mid-90's when the Lower East Side really stood for something)?

I was reminded of a friend of mine who was recently married and said that she knew she really loved her husband when she realized she would wipe his ass if he was too sick to do it himself. 'I've come home from a long day at work and looked at that man and not wanted to have sex with him,' she said. 'That's real love.'

It's like the cruelest part of romance is the mutual deceit, where two people agree to hallucinate some astral union together, through which divinity is revived and perpetually kept alive in the irreplaceably unique bond between them. The search for love teaches us to up-sell, to look forward and expect big things. Where are we headed? Where do we stand with each other? We're always rolling the ball up some delusional hill expecting to find a secret cache of fireworks at the top. What if the top of the hill is just an outhouse with a sick lover and a dirty ass that needs wiping? What if it's a dentist's chair?

I remember staring into my dentist's hazel eyes that afternoon, watching her pupils pivot around the corners of my mouth without even acknowledging how close I was to her. We were breathing the same air. Our noses were inches apart. She was telling me about her ruined relationships, her unsupportive parents, confessing impulses to cover loneliness with avarice. I saw her pale freckles and the creases in the skin beside her eyes. I looked at the veins on her hands, thickening and turning green with age. I felt a ridiculous affection for this woman. And a giddiness that I would be able to leave within the hour and not have to think about her at all for another six months.

Shave My Bush

I think it was pornography that first planted the idea of shaving my pubic hair in my teenage brain. 'Guys do it in porno because it makes their penises look bigger,' my friend told me with 15-year-old solemnity. I was still excited to just have pubic hair so the idea of trimming it back didn't seem intuitive. While shaving might make a penis look bigger, it doesn't actually make it bigger so his logic made even less sense to me. I finally started trimming back my mange in college when a new idea dawned on me: a manicured pubic lawn might make the penis seem more inviting, less like an overgrown junk heap of kinky Brillo.

In all the intervening years I haven't had any comment on my pubic hair, pro or con. One of the surprises of losing my virginity was just how nice the friction of pubic hair felt. Rocking away in the missionary position I was happily taken with all the little tugs and pulls as my pubic hair became entwined with, and separated from, my partner's pubic hair. No one had ever told me about that. It was nice.

A light trim of the penis awning has become a relatively normal part of many men's daily routines under the banner of 'manscaping.' For women, a full shave seems to be far more common than a discretely appointed six o'clock shadow. A fully shaved vagina is like a mounted deer head with a lot of my friends. It's a prized trophy that incites head nods with a lurid sneer of approval. That's what I'm talking about. Shave it all off. Nice.

It's easy to fetishize body parts with such an explicit role in sex, wanting to see them as nakedly as possible. There's certainly a large contingent of men who happily fixate on breasts. For me, sex resides in the face and the hips. Lips, eyes, chin, ears, butt, the uterine slope below the navel, the labia, inner thigh, perineum. Swoon. The way the bulges and curves come together, and open to the inner vaginal sanctum (or mucus canal, if you will) is the most arousing sexual image I can imagine. And it's hard to imagine it without hair.

I remember the first time I saw a vagina when I was a kid. My cousins were visiting and I saw one scamper from the guest room to the bathroom naked, getting ready to change into a bathing suit for an afternoon swimming session. I was in first grade. It was flat, hairless, monochromatic, and seemed almost without function. It was like looking at an alien artifact.

The first time I experienced a fully shaved vagina as an adult it reminded me of that moment. I became totally indifferent. All of the excitement I had been building up suddenly became disappointment. I felt like I was looking at an animatronic doll. It was as if someone had taken the hairy and rounded woman I thought I was sleeping with and replaced her with a perverse rubber molding. When I see a shaved vagina it reminds me instinctually of pre-pubescence and it's wholly uninteresting.

There is a bristling underbelly to male sexuality that celebrates that perversely young, the barely legal conquest. Popular music is riddled with men in tight pants alluding to the Roman delights of underage women, from John Lennon to Kip Winger. It's hard not to see an echo of that in the celebration of the shorn snatch. Which is not to suggest that those men exchanging smug glances about the excellence of a bare yoni are pedophiles. Men are blunt instruments, we celebrate our own depravity. We burp, we fart, we brag about 'getting' sex, and try to outmatch each other with how lewd we can be. Then we slink off to our bathrooms and shave our own balls, like some private act of consideration for those who might one day appreciate the forethought.

How to Pick Up Women

When I was in junior high my best friend would give me the names of the girls at his school that he thought were pretty.

I would go over to his house and call them while he listened, talking with the confidence of not knowing or caring about them. I hit it off with one girl and after our first conversation she asked me to keep calling her. So I did. We talked regularly for a month before an actual date was arranged.

She was going to see Three Men and a Little Lady with some of her friends at a theater across town. I convinced a couple of my friends to come with me. We had to convince my friend's brother to take us, which took a lot of whining and begging that, in turn, made us late for the movie. We snuck into the darkened theater ten minutes after it had started. We couldn't find the girls and decided to just watch the movie and meet them outside when it was over.

After a dramatic climax on an estate somewhere in the British countryside the lights came on and I nervously led my now-cranky friends outside. We had half a pack of Camel Lights and my friends grew irritated with my insistence on meeting these random girls before ducking into a side alley to smoke.

Towards the back of the exiting crowd I saw a group of four girls. One in the middle looked like a fuzzy approximation of the face I had seen in J's yearbook. I was already nervous, and as I saw them heading our way, still oblivious to our presence, my heart started throbbing and my palms tingled with new sweat.

Feeling like there was no way out, I took a few terrified steps into the crowd. As I came nearer C looked up and saw me. Her face went blank and it looked like her mouth fell open just a little bit. I thought that she might turn around and run back into the theater to seek refuge.

'Hey, I'm Mike,' I said as I stepped in front of them. C's friends started giggling. C looked me in the eye while her legs twisted against themselves.

'Hey,' she said.

I didn't know what else to say and after a few seconds of terrifying silence passed I asked her to come behind the theater with me and my friends to smoke cigarettes. I knew C liked to smoke, she stole her mother's menthols she'd told me one night over the phone.

C's face transformed from blank to incredulous. Her eyes narrowed and her lips parted in disbelief just before she started laughing in my face.

'No way,' she said. 'Why would I want to go smoke cigarettes with you?' she asked. She grabbed one of her friend's hands and started walking quickly away, saying she was late and had to get home even though it was summer and the middle of the afternoon.

Up until that point I had the self-loathing adolescent's hunch that everyone found me physically disgusting, and this was the irrefutable confirmation I had been waiting for.

It took a long time to realize that I was only revolting to some people, not all. It's always a surprise when I find people who are actually attracted to me. And it's even more of a surprise when I find myself together with someone I'm attracted to.

I'm not adept at picking up women, and I don't really try to. I resent the notion of seduction. I don't want to convince someone that they should be with me. If they're not interested from the outset then neither am I. But there are two general practices I've used when I'm attracted to someone, which I'll now share in sequential order:

1. Say Hello
2. Shut up

There are a lot of men who've applied endless thought and energy to the arithmetic of seduction. They've created a conversational roadmap that any man can use to make himself appear more desirable. The idea of following a conversation by rote or having a specific objective in mind while talking to someone doesn't really inspire my sense of romance. But saying hello to an attractive stranger does.

It's obvious, I realize, but how many people ever really act on attraction when they're out? How many people catch your eye every day, and how many do you try and connect with? It's easier to sit back and analyze a person, imagine who they are, look at what they're wearing, build up a safe fantasy, and then let it all evaporate in a poof as they walk out the door a few minutes later.

Deciding you're interested enough to risk rejection and embarrassment for the sake of saying hello to someone new is always worth it. Even in the crumbling flames of rejection, the knowledge that I tried has always been better company and comfort than inaction. Like everything else, you can worry that there's a right way and a wrong way to talk to somebody, that there's a formal set of standards for seductive conversation. But there isn't. You determine what's right and wrong, seductive or unappealing with each person you meet, and the standards are in constant flux.

The next step isn't as intuitive. I've been described as aloof since I was a teenager. I can be quiet and withdrawn, disappearing into a veneer of passive gazing. But I can also go on epic runs of motor-mouthing. It alleviates my anxiety to fill in all the silences with a gush of words. I have to force myself to talk less when I'm with someone new, to be comfortable with the presence of conversational slack.

I like to use conversation and wit to make a show of how much I like someone, and my speech can become slightly manic trying to rid myself of the tantalizing burden of the attraction. Instead, I am more attractive when I shut my mouth. When I'm out with someone I really like for the first time the thought that goes through my head more than any other is, 'Shut up, just shut up.'

It's hard to trust yourself when you're taking a chance with someone you're attracted to. You take the spotlight for a few minutes. You become the guy in the coffee shop or the dude in the vegetable aisle trying his luck with a woman. People are watching, people are eavesdropping; you're on stage and have to perform. When I feel strongly enough about a person, I'll force myself out in spite of the embarrassment, and then try to keep my mouth shut for as long as I can stand.

Breaking Up in a Text Message

I got my first cell phone when I was 28. One of my old college friends replied to the group email in which I sent out with my new number exclaiming that hell must have frozen over. I love talking on the phone for long drifts of time. I hate being the first one to say goodbye. A week after N left San Francisco she called me one night drunk from her mother's house, where she was staying for another few days before flying to New York. I thought it would be clever to send her a text message at the same that we were talking and so I pulled the phone away from my ear long enough to write 'I love you' into the blinking text line while she was telling a story. Neither of us wanted to hang up and so we fell asleep together over the phone. It felt like she wasn't quite so far away to hear the faint digitized rhythm of her drunken sleeping breath. In the morning I found my phone still open at my ear by the pillow, covered in drool and the battery dead.

Talking on the phone is patently confessional. I find myself fixating on a person's physical appearance just as much as I focus on their words when talking face-to-face. On the phone, I don't have to stare at the budding pimple just to the left of the ear lobe, or wonder if I'm making too much eye contact, then return again to the conversation only to try and play catch up.

Over the phone, all that extra energy can be focused on the voice, the timbre, the inflection, the stumbles, and the spastic I-don't-knows that serve as the connective tissue between unwilling sentences. When I was 14 I spent a night prank calling random numbers with my friend J. The last number I called, which formed the pattern of a right triangle on the number pad of my parents' phone, went through to the house of a girl I'd never met before. I heard a rounded and curious young voice answer and the joke I was about to tell suddenly seemed beside the point. I said the only other thing I could come up with. 'Hi.'

We spent an hour on the phone, revealing calculated tidbits about each other in little increments. I can't remember what we talked about, but I know it wound up being religiously-oriented (she went to a Christian high school, as it turned out). In the same way that something in her voice had subverted my faux-cocky bravura, there was something in her way of thinking, both direct and vulnerable, that attracted me to her. This was S, the first woman I ever fell in love with.

We spoke four or five times a week for more than two years. She would call me from the bathtub, soaking her sore muscles after color guard practice; we'd watch Melrose Place together over the phone; we'd shut out the lights and crawl into bed together, each in our own room, our words comfortably meandering past each other. We would talk for two and three hours at a time. I only saw her in person twice over those two years. We went on a date once (she had to drive because I didn't have a car), and I snuck onto the campus of her school to share lunch one day. That's it. When I was 16 she graduated from high school and moved away. I never spoke to her again.

Now that I have a cell phone, I send text messages like an amphetamized chimpanzee. Aside from convenience, it's irresistible to know that I can send someone any little message I want and touch their day almost instantly. I once broke up with a woman over text.

We met at a friend's birthday party. She had bleached blonde hair with a pink streak in it, which seemed out of place with her business-chic clothing. I was immediately attracted to her. We talked for a while, then I walked her to her car when she had to leave. She gave me her business card and a quick peck. We went out a week later. After a late dinner I walked her back to her car again, and we kissed for three hours steaming up the windows like it was prom night. Around 2AM some creaky old neighborhood watchman knocked on the window to make sure things were okay. 'Yeah, we're doing great. Thanks.'

She was a TV executive, a few years older than me, and had a busy schedule. I was working two jobs and trying to raise financing for a movie in my spare time. We still managed to see each other once a week. She used to tease me about how stoic I was. 'You're my little science experiment,' she would say to me. She had never dated a man as aloof as I was. When I come across as aloof with women, it usually means I don't trust them or fear them in some way.

We spent a very comfortable few months together with no pressure to discuss where things were going. Neither of us pressed to label what we were doing together. I liked her. I admired her. But there was something ridiculous about her. She made a lot of money and would freely use it to do things like hire a nutritionist to tell her what kinds of almonds to eat. I don't find that objectionable, but I knew that her way of living wouldn't ever be a way that I wanted to live.

I think of love as inevitable, a function of time and more than luck. I've discovered I can begin to love a person after sharing even just a small amount of time together. It's like I have love autism. After a few months, I started to feel it happening with H. I wasn't falling in love with her (a useless phrase stamped across a useful distinction), but my lazy affection was solidifying into something L-shaped. This made me deeply uncomfortable. I didn't want to love someone older than me, who spoke about the difference in four star hotels in Berlin versus London, and who paid someone to tell her what to eat.

I realized I had to stop seeing her. I didn't want to care for her any more than I already did. I didn't want to share the practical-ities of her life in a way that love would make inevitable (for me at least). So I started avoiding her calls. After a week of trading voicemails and some too-convenient scheduling conflicts she left for a business trip. When she came back I was working 12-hour days at a film market trying to convince toothy Canadian investors to give me half a million dollars to make a movie. She sent me texts over the first couple days of the market. I sent flat, minimalist replies.

On the third day of the market, all my meetings were over and nobody had been impressed with my pitch. I sat in a puffy armchair in the lobby of a Santa Monica hotel sipping coffee from a paper cup, thinking about work, salesmanship, convincing people to give you things. I got a text from her asking me if I wanted to meet for a drink later. I mashed my toes into the bottom of my shoes. 'No,' I thought to myself. 'I still have work to do.'

I wrote back to her that I couldn't, I had to go home and write instead. 'I see. Well then, write well.'

Rate My Penis Size

I was 19 when I was first considered the idea that the size of a man's penis might be meaningful in one way or another. I had joked about it for years growing up. There's a communal instinct among 13 and 14 year-old boys that leads them to brag about the eight inches of limpness dangling in their pants. It was an entirely absurd thing to say then, and I was astonished to consider, just a few short years later, that someone might actually think my lacking an eight-incher, or even a seven-incher, could somehow be a real negative. Could the length and girth of my unconsidered appendage really be a reason for a woman not liking me?

So much of the male ego is bound up in competition. We play little league, line up according to height, race each other in PE class, wrestle in the school yard just to see who's the most dominant. Men are subconsciously driven by a fear of inade-quacy in front of their peers. Fine scientists everywhere will confirm this is rooted in evolutionary pressures of competing for a mate and proving oneself to be a macho provider in the Pleistocene wastes.

When it comes to strength or intelligence, there are a huge number of ways a man can go about improving himself. With penis size, the universe has either blessed you in full or damned you to a lifetime of lowered expectations. So it's predictable, I suppose, that penis size comes to be a harbinger of psychic dysfunction in a man's life. I once read the following anonymous confessional, presumably a man complaining about his girlfriend: 'We don't talk about anything meaningful, I hate your friends, you are not smart, and I can't walk around campus without seeing somebody who's had u too. Basically, you are a slut.'

Not being satisfied with the way you communicate and not

getting along with your partner's friends are two great reasons to question any relationship. Calling someone a slut because you're uncomfortable with the number of partners she's had is so hopelessly vulnerable it makes me wince. Sex can be a lot of things, and treating it as some proprietary metaphor for a person's moral rectitude is pathetic. Would you hold your lover accountable for all the intimate conversations she's had with someone else, or all the times she's laughed at another man's jokes?

The need to dismiss a woman based on the number of partners she's had seems to more likely to be penis inadequacy masquerading as morality. It sounds like a man irrationally afraid that one of those lovers that's been so freely accepted and tossed aside might have a bigger member. And this will have to be the fault of the woman. Only a whore would need so much dong in her life.

The maddening thing about this fear of inadequacy is that there's no good ways for a typical straight man to set his mind at ease. Statistics tell us the average penis size is six inches long and the average vagina four inches deep. The pornography that I've been watching since I was 15 tells me something different. After those tense moments in the high school gym showers, straight men rarely get to see penises outside of pornography. As Freud noted, the things that frighten us most are the things that we subconsciously draw closest to. It makes sense that porn penises should all be so big since the majority of viewers are men. We want to torture ourselves.

I used to be sure that I had a small penis, that there was something fundamentally inadequate about it. The shape was all wrong, it was too skinny, it didn't go deep enough. Looking down on my shriveled penis in the shower some mornings I wondered at how small and acorn-like the thing had become. How could someone with an appendage of such retreating proportions ever hold his head up in public? Of course the truth is entirely unremarkable. My penis is a six-inch erection, curvy, and a bit thicker than my index and middle finger put together.

The things in our life don't speak for us anymore than we allow them to. If sex is mechanics in exclusivity, than size and inter-departmental compatibility are paramount. If sex is a process of sharing your truest self with another, then your whole life can become an erotic prompt. You can always orchestrate a new position or get a new toy, but you can't fake the experience of being with someone who you know isn't holding anything back. Being with a woman who hasn't allowed some draconian heritage of penis envy to dictate her search for love and intimacy should make a man feel lucky. And yet it very often just makes us feel small.

On Your Own, or Moving On

I'm bad at letting go. When I was a kid my grandpa gave me 500 Danish crowns one summer. It was a lot of money and I wanted to treat it solemnly. I couldn't imagine buying something like a toy or candy with it, though those were the only things I really wanted at the time. I saved it instead. I took it back to America, thinking I would wait until there was something really special to use it on, something that would then become a physical keepsake of my grandpa. I put the bill into a book, keeping it pressed and in perfect condition.

Years went by and I couldn't think of anything to buy, the longer I waited the more attached I became to the bill itself. Soon it looked less like money and more like an ornate shred of art, I could see all the little dotted lines swirling around to form the picture of royalty. The bill itself started to become the keepsake and I never spent it. Once it became symbolic, I couldn't deal with the idea of converting it into something other than what it was.

I got a new cell phone a few months after N left. In moving everything over from my old phone I encountered one hurdle. I can only bring around thirty of my saved text messages from my old phone. Which is a problem because I've got close to a hundred old texts, received and sent, that I've held onto like little emotional trinkets.

Most of the texts are from N. I sent a text to my friend P on Saturday to see if he knew a way I could save all the old texts intact and he immediately sniffed out what I was doing. 'Do you really think that's a good idea?' he wrote me back. 'What's that going to accomplish?' I've got lots of saved stuff, I protested, not just from her.

There's one text I got from J two years ago. 'The avocados are freezing but it is good for the wine, life is good.' I remember the night she sent it to me. We spent the first few months of our friendship hooking up here and there. I started to fall for her and took her out for dinner one night (which consisted of a cheese plate and a few glasses of wine). I told her I wanted to be her boyfriend, though I was careful to phrase it in an adult way with lots of parentheticals and qualifiers. 'That's not going to happen,' I remember her telling me.

A few months later, I remember getting that text late one weeknight. I was sitting at the desk in my bedroom working. The text came unprompted, a small reminder of the lingering fondness still between us. So I saved it, to remember that moment we had, which was left behind. A little rag taken out of time, from a place I used to be but can't go back to.

I've created folders in my email account to save old messages from women in my past. I've still got a banker's box in the closet that has the one letter I ever got from S, the first girl I fell in love with. She wrote it to me from a summer school class while she was trying to learn how to type. The whole thing was printed in dot matrix, except for her signature, which had a little heart looped into the cursive.

Now I have a dilapidated flip phone with a bunch of old text messages trapped inside, little flags, moments that I might otherwise have forgotten by now. Looking back over them, trying to figure out which should be deleted, I remember again one of the last nights N was here. I rented a car and drove into the countryside to see her at her mother's one last time. We stayed up until 5AM, walking by the house she grew up in, seeing the deli where the Russian vendor used to give her free piroshki because she was so pretty.

When the sky started to lighten it was time to go. I drove back into the city, feeling like I was in a narcoleptic quicksand, trying to keep awake just long enough for the hour drive to the rental place. After I dropped off the car, I stumbled into the BART and rode back to my neighborhood. As I sat down I sent her a text, saying that I had survived the drive and was safely returned. I closed my eyes and leaned my head against the glass window and put my iPod on shuffle. I remember the song that was playing, something I hadn't heard in years, 'Gates of the Garden' by Nick Cave. I started crying. It felt like I was losing an organ, but there was no physical pain, it was all brain sadness and numb body.

A week earlier, I sent her an entire sonnet in a text ('to love that well which thou must leave ere long'). I remember sitting at my desk after lunch, copying three lines into a single text, then saving it as a draft so I could copy the other lines and send the whole thing at once. I made sure to start with the last three lines and work back to the beginning so that she could read it in order. The first time she told me she loved me, it was in a text message.

Before I got my new phone I hadn't looked at any of those old texts in months and then I had to start deleting them. I don't want to let them go.

'Still think you are cool :-)' I remember the night she sent it to me. I remember the one I sent to her that it was responding to. Click. Now it's gone.

Rate my Blowjobs

I was out at a bar with a friend one night. This friend is a neurotic catastrophe (I don't mean that in a negative way) but has one saving grace: he's really good looking. He's a tall, brawny, tanned work of physical symmetry. He's also a warbling gyroscope of emotional issues, but never you mind about that. There'll be time for those later. The benefit of going out to bars with him is that the frequency of being approached by random women increases terrifically compared to what I would experience on my own. And it reminds me that hitting on people is stupid. This is a prejudice I've had for a long time. It treats attraction and the metaphysics of romantic affinity as if they were a sport that could be won or lost through the application of skill.

So this night a feisty blonde woman came up to A and I, and inserted herself into our conversation. Small talk was exchanged, some pretense was created to explain her approach (it's always 'Don't I know you?') and it wasn't long before she had convinced us to take a sugary shot of something in the cranberry-watermelon family. Then she started telling us – I suppose I'm being generous at this point since most of this was directed at A, but indulge me for a few paragraphs—about what great blowjobs she gives. 'It's true,' she swore. 'You can ask any of my ex-boyfriends.'

I have never before met a stranger who tried to sell themselves based on sexual references. It might actually have been interesting to call her ex-boyfriends and talk about what her sexual pros and cons really were. But it's hard to be so clever on the spot, especially in the kind of a bar where people in pressed Banana Republic shirts dance with each other, waving hands over heads like elementary school kids awkwardly doing calisthenics. Next she asked us if we liked blowjobs.

How do you respond when someone asks you if you like oral

sex? In my defensive and overly-intellectual posture, I think of sex as communication more than performance. It's great with people that you care about and increasingly uncomfortable with people you don't have any deeper interest in. Some of the best mechanical sex I've had has been during one-night stands. Drawn out sessions of gymnastic vigor, that shakes the walls and leaves your bed humped off into a crooked angle halfway across the bedroom. These are also some of the experiences in my life that I'd just as soon not repeat. It's the depressing embodiment of small talk given a physical form. What can your body really have to say to a stranger beyond the pantomime of connection and feigned investment?

There are always the strange smells of breath, armpits, and sweat to remind you of the relative foreignness of that body in bed with you. There are always physical quirks to reconcile with: toenails, moles, the sourness of the inner ear, stubble, acne, the oddness of hands. None of these are physically revolting, but they're so uniquely personal they always remind me of how wholly unknown the person I'm with is. And finally, the mechanics of sex aren't all that mysterious after all. Our under-pants-areas are over-generous with nerve endings; it shouldn't be any great selling point for a grown person to be proud of their ability to produce pleasure in them. If you can manage to get me off just by biting my love handles, then I might admit rhetorical defeat on the point, but being good at blowjobs is like saying you're good at making sandwiches. I didn't realize it was all that mysterious a process.

All of which got me thinking about 'The Brown Bunny,' Vincent Gallo's movie about getting a blowjob from Chloe Sevigny. It's about more than that, but that climactic scene where two celebrities consent to share the mechanics of their sex with the world at large is as direct a statement as any about the movie. Blowjobs come and go, but the people giving them are irreplaceable. Gallo's character can't stop reliving his last sexual encounter with his now-dead wife because sex is the only language we have to begin to articulate what it feels like to love somebody. You can use words, or images, or sounds, but the truest and most direct expression of love is physical. Sex is language and vocabulary.

Which brings me back to a bar in the Mission, drunk on fruit juice and vodka, trying to reconcile what it was about this woman who insisted on pitching her sexual acumen to a couple of random guys in a bar. What would we really have to say to each other physically? The gears and spokes might run together, but to what end? I assume I'm a total anomaly in this regard. I've got several friends with libidos that reach into the stars and take great relish in the variety and intensity of their new sexual encounters. I envy them. I respect them fundamentally. But I don't think I understand their language.

The 45-Minute Walkout

One night I met a woman for drinks and after 45 minutes of terse chitchat she got up and walked away. 'You know what, I think I'm just going to leave,' she said as she looked from me to her empty wine glass and back again.

My first clue that things weren't going to go well came when she vetoed my idea of going to a peach-colored yuppie bar to play Stranger Chicken (in which you take turns giving your companion dares to approach strangers and perform goofy tasks—bum a cigarette, grab an ass, convince them you're an astronaut ...). Both the bar in question and the activity aren't to everyone's taste, but I thought it would be a fun way to spend a Friday night, whether or not we hit it off. Veto.

We agreed on meeting in some hipster alcove where conversation can be subconsciously guided by the defeated wobble of a Pavement song on the jukebox. I was unenthused about the prospect of a 'conversation' date, but went along for the ride. Nobody knows anything, after all. Especially when meeting strangers from the internet for a drink. I got to the bar a little early and, as instructed in her email, waited outside for her to arrive. I eavesdropped on three grad students talking about professors while smoking cigarettes. I debated for a minute about asking for a cigarette. K came riding up on a bicycle a few minutes later. I recognized her as she pulled up and gave her smile. 'How are you?' I asked.

This was the next bad sign. She raised her eyebrows in acknowledgement and didn't say anything, instead walking her bike a few feet past me to lock it up. This told me two things: I am less interesting than sticking a key in a U-lock; and I am not worth stepping out of K's comfort zone on a first date. Once K arranged her bike we walked inside. I was already thinking things would have to get better. There had to be a rebound coming at some point. I thought I was being overly analytical. There were probably dozens of reasons why our first impressions were going so badly, none of which needed be personal.

Inside, we stood at the bar deliberating on drinks in relative silence. K did not want to drink chardonnay or Budweiser. She settled on Pinot Grigio. I ordered a Manhattan. She got her wine first and headed back to the booth we had claimed on entering. I stood at the bar for another two minutes waiting for my drink to be made. This was strike three. As I turned and started walking towards the booth I could almost see the ghostly letters strung out in neon above our table, 'Abandon all hope, ye who enter here...'

As we started talking it seemed like K was offended by everything I said. I told her that Japantown creeped me out because it felt too white-bread. 'But it's filled with Japanese people,' she informed me. It wasn't a literal presence of white people that made my toes squirm, I elaborated, more the upscale hygienic quality the neighborhood had. The wide streets, clean restaurants with A ratings. The conspicuous absence of homeless people.

K wondered if I liked homeless people shooting up on my doorstep or passed out on the sidewalk in my neighborhood. I did, in fact. It's not that poverty is such a great thing, but it's an inevitable face of humanity that should be a part of any urban area. We are stupid and fallible creatures. Homeless people are a reminder that there isn't a net beneath us when we stupidly and fallibly fall.

As I went through all of this, boring myself, K kept taking big gulps of wine every time it looked like she was about to say something. I laughed at her. 'You don't like any of this, do you?' I said.

Then we landed on poetry. She asked me where I was from. 'Fresno,' I said. She arched her eyebrows and took another gulp of wine. If you're unfamiliar, the central valley is to San Francisco what New Jersey is to New York; an execrable backwater. After inoculating herself against what I might come up with next, she asked me what growing up in Fresno was like. 'It was okay,' I said. There were bad parts, but good ones too. There is, and has been, a rooted poetry scene there for decades (Phil Levine, David St. John, Larry Levis, Gary Soto...).

I told her that poetry is a dead medium. I love it, write it, read it, buy it, attend its public incantations. And still, the flame is dying, there's nothing left to say in poetry that will ever matter to more than a handful of people. Things have moved on to film (on its way out too), TV, music, interactivity. This went over even less well than the thought about the homeless people. Apparently she still has friends who go to poetry slams and have plenty of interesting things left to say with the medium.

Okay.

'I feel like you're talking at me, not to me,' she finally said after running out of wine. Hmmm. Here we go then, the end is near. I'm sure everything I was saying was about as interesting as comparing wood chip prices in a Home Depot. I had lost interest myself almost before I opened my mouth. And still, I didn't want to retreat. She had asked me questions, and I wanted to answer them honestly. Few people want honesty on a first date. It's a pretty idea, but an ugly thing in reality. We all have our own little kingdoms of truth and nobody likes to be reminded of those walls in the first hour of having met a person.

K looked at her empty glass. There was nothing left to say. I didn't have any questions for her. She seemed to have a mountain of words for me, but none that she wanted to let loose for fear of instigating a confrontation.

And so she got up, thanked me for the drink, and walked out the door.

Hitting Snooze on the Morning After

I'm terrible at waking up. I set two alarms and spend at least half an hour hitting the snooze button until the absolute last drip of sleep has been extracted from my warm morning bed. This is a pretty embarrassing habit to have when someone is sleeping over. It's terrible to share a bed with someone soft and warm and then hear the harsh blare of talk radio coming from one side of the bed, and then the staccato jingle of my cell phone alarm from the other a few minutes later. Variating between the two for 20 or 30 minutes, like a languorous cat trying to figure out the world's simplest Rube Goldberg contraption, has to leave a bad impression.

Mornings are a generally embarrassing time for me. In addition to torturing myself with alarms, I tend to look like a train wreck right when I get out of bed. A few years ago my friend P surprised me from out of town, knocking on my door early one morning while I was still asleep. When I opened the door, bleary-eyed and in my underpants, the first words out of his mouth were 'Are you alright? You look pretty rough.'

I was fine, but I sleep hard. My eyes grow dark pits underneath them and my skin loses its pallor as my blood pressure drops in dreaming. I also have a mangy head of hair that tends to exaggerate its spastic shape after a full night upon a pillow. I'm also prone to morning breath. I'm sure, in fact, my mouth is like a rank cavern most mornings.

I do a short workout in the mornings, which is also pretty silly looking. I do a cycle of pushups, leg raises, and some boxing with light weights before work every day (the avoidance of which is another good reason to stay in bed a few minutes longer – who wants to do ab exercises first thing in the morning?). Through the course of this routine I make all sorts of ridiculous faces and bizarre breathing noises as I try and squeeze out those last few reps. I can only imagine how preposterous that must look to someone cozily half asleep in my bed.

This routine might be cute for the first few weeks or months. It might be pleasantly irritating in the same way that it's nice to be teased a little by someone you're attracted to. It's easy to run away with the wildness of being attracted to someone new, and a few comic reminders they aren't as idealized as you might imagine can be comforting.

But after the early romance has outgrown its puppy dog years and become a full-grown beast, all those eccentricities gain a dull weight. Putting up with your man's snoring, or his 30 minutes of alarm jockeying every morning must inevitably turn into a galling watermark of how high the infatuated wave was when it broke, leaving behind the crass reality of a man in his underwear moving around half awake at seven in the morning.

My friend L suggested to me that I was torturing myself with the erector set of alarms I was relying on everyday. It's true. Trying to squeeze a few extra minutes of sleep out of a prematurely ended night is hopeless. Forcing someone else to listen to the drawn out blare of the alarm just because I wanted to put off the pain of waking on a Tuesday with a whole week still lying ahead is all wrong. It's the kind of lazy sufferage that is so easy to lay on someone else as soon as they're close enough to hear. Worse still, I look like a marmot wrestling an octopus when I work out. Would you hold that against me?

Come on My Face

It's hard to know whether pornography preceded certain socio-sexual habits, or whether normal people invented them. Sperm-swallowing is a practice I've rarely encountered in my sexual partners, but I've always found it sweet when it's happened to me. I've never pulled out and come on someone.

I feel ridiculous when I pull out. After all of the intense and dilated ascendency of sex—without a condom through impatience or mutual agreement of some sort—the man reaches his limit and manages to remove himself just in time to spill his spoutum on fallow turf. The well-timed pull out must surely have been practiced by generations of randy men, precocious students, and willow-eyed cock-painters.

More recently, the pull out has become a requirement of most all straight pornography. It's the pay-off, the visual punctuation for the vicarious masturbator. Whenever I've been in a position to come on another person I always feel an uncomfortable parallel with porn. When I feel myself closing in on the ejaculatory pivot point without a condom, I feel dilemmafied.

Coming is not an ending point or some desirable peak of sex to me. It's nice and all, but it's not a big part of what I want out of my time another naked person, so the more energy I have to spend thinking about what will happen when I do come is distracting. Especially when thinking about it evokes all sorts of expulsive imagery of porn men milking their scepters onto the fleshy landing pad of a woman's breasts or face. I can't handle thinking of myself in that way, and I'm even less interested in thinking about someone I'm sleeping with in that way.

For all the social rhetoric to the contrary, there's something instinctually derogatory in porn. There are a lot of crafty ways to rationalize pornography as empowerment, but I have a wince-reflex when I think about it. It seems to actually be most effective when it's most derogatory. All the Vaseline-lit softcore porn feels unnatural and alien. The athletic grinding and animalistic hammer sessions seem to be the most honest to me. I've lately found some porn that's openly derogatory to men.

There is something called 'Fuck Team Five,' in which groups of Amazonian porn star women roam the streets looking for regular guys to sleep with. They have quick rabbit sex with convenience store clerks, chubby mechanics, and dorky comic book nerds. They emasculate the homely, make fun of the guys with small penises, or the ones who can't get an erection.

When I think of pulling out and coming on someone I feel the same insinuation of macho dominance and conquest, and a simultaneous sense of physical degradation of the hapless man wooed by strangers in a grocery store parking lot – simultaneously gratified and ridiculed.

After I moved to New York I didn't masturbate for a long period, more than a week. When I finally did return to the act, I came all over myself – my chest, my chin, my navel, my thighs. It was a mess. And it felt nice. The warm come was soft and velveteen as it pooled over my skin. It felt strangely gentle and modest, only a few ounces of bodily fluid. It smelled neutral; it probably smelled like me.

Bodily fluids are a good litmus test for attraction. When someone's leakings disgust you, odds are good you're not really attracted to them. When you really want someone, thinking about their saliva, vaginal fluid, sweat, period, come, pre-ejaculate; it all elicits some carnal hunger. We're taught to be ashamed of our bodies and their functioning. These are private areas, and personal zones, dirty to share with someone else.

The idea that coming on someone is degrading implies that there's something dirty or improper in coming; that a nice, normal woman wouldn't want all that foul man-splatter on her body.

I never imagined that it could be nice and sweet; just another part of yourself to share with someone you really, really like. Then I realized I'd been coming on myself all these years and never stopped to appreciate how nice it really was.

The Wine Bar as the End of Civilization

I once made the irreversible mistake of going on a date at a wine bar. It's bad enough meeting someone for drinks, as if the presence of alcohol can somehow counterbalance the fact that neither of you could come up with something more amusing than drinking at a table to interview one another. Wine bars are the worst possible location for a date so formal and uninspired.

Wine bars are corrupt temples of conspicuous consumption. They're about appreciating the arcana of labels and the security of assimilating with the dictums of some higher authority's assurances of quality. The snobbery of only serving wine is a passive-aggressive apology for having to stoop so low as to serve alcohol in the first place. I like drinking wine, but I don't think it needs to be its own exclusionary activity, taking place in metro-politan back alleys with names that invariably involve the word 'hotel.'

Moreover, I like drinking. I like the wastefulness of buying expensive champagne and booze that comes with illegible family crests on the label. But I wouldn't do it if I didn't get drunk. I also like buying cans of malt liquor that come with bright orange stickers that say '$2.25' or '$1.79.' Being drunk feels good, and this makes drinking a perfect social activity. Who wouldn't want to spend as much time as possible feeling good in the company of other people? So why make that process of getting drunk and socializing an affair that celebrates social stratification? Is that a hint of cantaloupe? Unusual for a Shiraz. Here's fourteen dollars.

So but anyway, there I was drinking something bubbly and Spanish, chatting with a cute marine biologist with an Audrey Hepburn haircut and a teal sundress hanging loosely against her browned skin. I was attracted to this woman, but I kept zoning out as she explained her job. It wasn't long before we were talking about Jeffrey Sachs and how everyone in international development is doing it wrong. When I sensed a long monologue coming on, I let my mind wander. 'Is this a bad date?' I kept wondering.

I was attracted to her; enough at least. We seemed to have similar interests, and played well together, alternately speculating about how to fix Congo and cure AIDS. I might as well have been talking to a long-lost uncle at some distant relative's wake. I kept thinking that I should kiss her. 'Maybe that will snuff out this long string of baseless anecdotes,' I thought. We saw an opening on a couch across the bar and moved from our barstools. As I walked behind her I noticed what a big and round butt was hiding underneath her dress. It occurred to me that she had a grandmother's ass, though I don't really know where that idea came from, aside from the vague associations with plumpness. This detail led quite directly to thoughts of sex.

Thinking about sex with your date after an hour of dry conversation is probably a bad sign, especially when you're not listening very carefully to anything they say. Feeling that kind of inarticulate attraction to my date while still managing to be totally bored by her was awkward and surprising, like getting an erection in the middle of a meeting at work. I realized we were bullshitting each other. Running our mouths about stuff that seemed like it fit in the formal equation of our first date, in the same way that asking the bartender for an 'earthy' Italian red seemed appropriate. It wasn't actually this woman that I was attracted to, it was the insinuation of something underneath her wispy clothes that had launched my imagination. I wasn't thinking about her at all.

After another hour of limpid conversation I started yawning. She did too. 'Do you want to go somewhere else?' she asked. 'I got up pretty early this morning, but I will if you want to,' I said.

'No, I'm pretty tired too.'

Things came to an end with a hug and a kiss on the cheek at her car. We should have taken forties to the park and played

Stranger Chicken into the waxy hours of the night. I'm never going on another first date at a wine bar again.

Some Corner in Brooklyn

I don't know how to write this one. I went to New York for a few days at the end of summer, three months after N had moved there. I had spent a week in Denmark visiting my family. My grandmother has Alzheimer's disease and my grandfather died the winter before and we had to put her into a nursing home. I spent a week in Denmark helping to clean out my grandparent's house to get it ready for sale. On the way back, I stopped in New York to visit my friend P, who I've known since high school and then lived in a midtown neighborhood that resembled an outdoor mall. But I was there to see N, the rest was only pretext.

It was the first time I had been to New York since I was 16. I used to think I would move to New York after high school when I had ambitions of becoming a rockstar/teenage novelist. I decided to go to college in Los Angels instead, and wound up working in the movies for a few years before going to Peace Corps, and suddenly it had been ten years since the last time I ever seriously thought about New York.

I spent my days there walking around the city randomly. P had to work during the day so I would find a subway station and take it in some direction. I'd get off when I could no longer recognize the station names and try to figure out how to walk back to P's apartment. When I was in Peace Corps I realized one of my favorite things in life is waking up in a foreign place with no real understanding of where I am. Every experience can be improvised, remaining perpetually new and challenging.

I don't know where the compulsion to be in long-term relationships comes from. I can't remember a time when I didn't picture myself in one at the butt-end of an idealized fantasy of how my life would unspool. It was assumed, like a birthright or some act of infantile mimicry, aping the shape of my parents' lives. I've fallen in love five times. When I was younger I wondered what the point of sticking with a person long-term could possibly be since things all seemed to end in the same way: age, defeat, and regression.

I was always completely serious about the possibility of a shared life with each of the women I was variously in love with. Still, there was a murmur of compromise running underneath each one. I would have taken a blind leap of faith because the love was real and I was young and jumping was instinctual. What else can you do when you're 24 and in love? There's something impossibly erotic and thrilling about picking up the weight of your entire life and flinging it over the edge of a metaphysical promise with some young tender who smiles in slow motion. Looking back, part of what made the prospect exciting then was the subconscious understanding that none of it was right.

I could sense the reasons why things would never work out in the long-term with each woman, but the adrenaline and the hubris of the moment, following in the wake of my parents and their parents, was irresistible. Falling in love was like picking a major in college. It was untethered experimentation based on some intense feelings without any knowledge of how durable and seaworthy they would remain after a few semesters of tough prerequisites.

I've never been in love in the way I was with N. She's the love of my life. It's scary writing that in black and white, assigning specific words to something so totally ineffable. When I was younger I remember hearing an aphorism about falling in love on a sitcom rerun. There are three loves in life: your first love, your true love, and the one you wind up with. I've had to let go of lots of love, but it always made sense underneath it all. It was never right. I've never had to let go of something that was right, that was like a discovery of a part of myself I didn't know was there. And then it was there. For a little while.

N moved to New York for a few reasons, the most insurmountable of which was her boyfriend. She had taken a vacation to New York, where she had lived after college. During this period she reconnoitered with this on-again off-again man, discovering some remnant magic had survived their bi-coastal interregnum. When she came back to San Francisco, she announced that she was going to move to New York to get back together with her boyfriend. We met a month later. Every experience we had together took place in the darkening shadow of her coming move. We could fall in love easily because it was certain we could not have a future together.

I called her when I landed in New York and we made plans to meet for happy hour. I spent the day wandering around Harlem, trying to pretend there was nothing especially exciting about to happen. Inside I felt like a dog in a pen hopping manically after having heard the promising tinkle of a leash. I found her at five, stationary and smoking in mass of rush hour workers who had some other place to be, unaware that the block they were pushing through was, in fact, the apotheosis of all human hope and the reconciliation of the irreconcilable broken halves.

She had gotten skinnier and looked intimidatingly grown up, dispassionate in a pressed gray shirt, tight black jeans, and severe high heels. I felt faintly clownish in pink and gold sneakers, hair frizzy and ballooning outward in the August humidity, a sharp note of cologne covering the salty pelt scent that a day spent walking had given me. We hugged, smiling half-smiles. I wanted to pick her up, to feel her entire weight straining against my muscles, to swallow her with my arms. Instead, I leaned down and gave her a soft squeeze, making sure to not press my dewy body against hers too revoltingly. We walked to a bar nearby, decorated like a kitschy hunting lodge, and sat outside in a sunken back patio, walled in by tall, 100 year-old buildings and the wooly hot air still trapped between them.

We caught up, shyly working through the long list of recent events that had thoughtlessly accumulated after three months of living separate lives in separate cities. We smoked lots. I gave her a taxidermy owl with one eye missing, something my grandparents had bought long ago, and which I'd rescued from a back room in my Uncle's house in Denmark. I'd always known her to love taxidermy (when she moved I very briefly considered buying her a two chicks conjoined at the head and posed in a bell jar, which she'd once commented on in a store window, an $800 souvenir of our love, something that I feared would forever stamp me as a gullible idiot, chasing after love with immoderate shows of money).

Later some of my friends met us and we all went out to dinner. We snuck outside to smoke mid-meal. 'I missed you,' I told her. 'I missed you too.' I hugged her again and we stood like that for a minute, quietly, cigarettes wasting their smoky little bodies between our fingers.

After dinner we went back to P's house to drink more. We sat in the open window of his 8th floor high-rise, above the inconsiderate blare of Herald Square. Then P went to bed and our other friend disappeared, and we were alone on P's couch, drunk, listening to Roxy Music. We passed out together, our bodies forming a right angle on the L-shaped couch, the tops of our heads pressed together, holding hands over them.

Her phone kept buzzing in her purse. I tried to wake her. She was, no doubt, wanted back home, her presence with me had a reciprocal absence in another room somewhere across the river. I didn't want her to get in trouble (it's true, if you can believe that). But she wouldn't wake up, and so we spent the night on the couch. I I tried to stay awake as long as I could, feeling the warmth of her hand in mine, softly pressing against her head, listening to her breath, periodically breaking into snores, clunky snatches of air snorting through her delicate bouche.

In the morning, a painful gray smog in the air and the painful footsteps of old booze and cigarettes still drying in my brain, she sat up and reviewed the messages waiting in her phone. I heard a long exhale and became aware that she was sitting above me. I opened my eyes and saw her looking down at me, her hair creating a wavy confessional around her face. I closed my eyes again. She leaned down and kissed me softly.

Then she stood up and left. She was leaving town that morning, a weekend was to be spent in the mountains with her boyfriend's relations. After she went home to pack, inventing some excuse of having gotten too drunk and passing out on her girlfriend's couch, we met again in Washington Square Park for bagels and hangover cigarettes. Then we rode the subway to Port Authority and she slipped through the sliding doors and I was alone.

The next day, I was lost in Brooklyn somewhere. I had taken a series of wrong turns from the subway station and wound up in Bed Stuy and then Fort Greene. After a while I made it to Williamsburg, though it was some wide-laned industrial area that didn't seem like the orgiastic hipster hive I'd thought it would be. My phone rang when I was at the corner of 14th and Wythe. It was N. She had snuck off for a walk alone in the woods to call me. I sat down and leaned against the red brick workshop building, staring at a man in cut-off shorts and a fedora trying to fix an old minivan across the street. It was August, humid and hot. I had a backpack and had been sweating. I could feel the plastic heat of the phone against my cheek.

Twenty minutes later, I hung up the phone. Across the street I saw a rusty old door, the word 'faile' painted on it in a pastel shade of purple, a small heart dotting the 'i.' Two men biked by, with giant messenger bags on their backs. The man across the street worked on his minivan. I was crying.

Your Mom Will Do

I went on a cruise with my parents and older brother after he finished medical school. My parents decided that we should all spend seven days in a floating hotel sailing down the coast of Baja, Mexico. I had never been on a cruise and I wasn't looking forward to breaking that cherry with my parents in tow. The idea of being trapped in a giant metal boat with room service and closed circuit television didn't sound like an ideal way to spend a week. But sometimes you have to close your eyes and take a leap of faith for the sake of the group, and so I went.

The only thing I was looking forward to was the possibility of having an open bar on every deck. I understood that everything charged to my room key in magical ship-bucks would eventually show up on my credit card statement, but I decided that should be no cause for moderation. My parents would enjoy the historical lectures and ballroom dancing, my brother would gamble in the casino, and I would prowl the disco all night ordering drinks by color rather than name.

The stereotypes people have about cruises are true. The only choices for companionship are old people and hormone frenzied 19-year-olds. This was distressingly apparent on the first night in the distressingly-named Neptune disco, where all the 19-year-old boys in new white sneakers and saggy cargo shorts huddled on one side of the dance floor and all the sunburned girls in mini skirts and flip flops danced to the Backstreet Boys on the other side. It was like being stuck in a giant awkward silence between two factions who were clearly ogling each other.

Amidst the hesitant groundwork being laid for 19-year-old rabbit sex, I found a pretty blonde woman who seemed more appropriate for my demographic (I had just turned 25). She had just graduated from USC and was on a celebrating that feat with her parents. She was at the disco with her mother, a frisky-looking 55-year-old with a graying bob. I started to talking to the daughter (I can't even remember her name anymore), and we hit things off well enough. She was coy and aloof. She kept her body perpendicular to mine, but her eyes would linger over me a little longer than necessary when we spoke.

I asked her and her mother to come out and dance with me. They offered faux-protests while they walked to the dance floor and soon we were gyrating in a sea of 19-year-olds. Around 1AM they retired back to their room so that Dad/Husband wouldn't get too worried. For the remainder of the cruise, I kept bumping into the daughter and her mother. They were always traveling in tandem. We would see each other at the formal dinners, wandering around the outer deck, poking through the library, at the disco.

I was attracted to the daughter, but I didn't know how to separate her from her mother. I thought she was attracted to me, but she didn't go out of her way to extricate herself from her mother's company. I felt awkward about pressing too hard for a more formal 'date,' if such a thing can be had on a cruise. So our interactions remained hygienically fun and photogenic. We must have looked like that perpetually smiling clump of cruise-goers reveling in a brochure.

I became more and more restless as the cruise wore on. The claustrophobia began to set in, as well as a lurking dissatisfaction that the only things I was doing were eating, drinking, and whiling away afternoon hangovers on the pool deck reading John Fante. I started to feel like I was in an R-rated hamster cage. I remember one morning, after an athletic night of drinking and dancing in the Neptune: before my eyes opened I was aware of a nauseating sway on all sides. Then the distressingly fuzzy hangover ache settled over me, my nerves shot from a night of alcohol-induced adrenaline flow, my brain cramping, my mouth dry and scratchy. Suddenly the blankets felt heavy and too hot. I opened my eyes and everything was perfectly black. There was no bedside clock and no light creeping in from anywhere. I had no idea where I was.

I sat up and put my hand out against the far wall. I could hear my brother's sleep-breathing a few feet away. I followed my hand down the wall to the bathroom door. For whatever reason I didn't want to turn on the light and instead felt my way to the toilet lid. I lifted it and started pissing. I felt dizzy, my head started to tingle with the sudden blood rush from standing up. The boat swayed. I felt my knees buckle, and a grayish white flashed behind my eyes. Then somehow I was on the floor, in total darkness, my shorts around my ankles, everything around me swaying. I had no idea what time of day it was. If there is a hell somewhere in the universe, it must be something like this.

From that moment forward I realized I needed to get off the boat. And there was no way off.

On the last night of the cruise I saw the daughter and her mother in the casino in the early evening. We stopped and talked for a few minutes. I asked the daughter if she wanted to meet me alone in one of the bars later. She hesitated, made some vague excuses. She said she liked me, but she couldn't leave her mom since it was the last night on-board. I had no idea what she was trying to say. It frustrated me that we had spent a whole week chatting, dancing, and goofing off, and now she was pulling back.

That night at the disco I ignored the daughter completely. I spoke only to the mother. A ballad came on and I asked the mother to dance. I was on my way to being very drunk. I nestled my chin against the mother's shoulder as we danced. I whispered into her ear, 'You're so beautiful.' I felt her body react, not quite a shudder but a simultaneous loosening and tensing. 'Stop it,' she said.

I nuzzled my nose against her ear, and started to nibble on the lobs softly. She inhaled through her nose and leaned her head into mine. I let the tip of my tongue run along the lower edge of her ear, then bit down on it. I looked back to the table where the daughter sat by herself, sipping a drink and watching. I kissed the mother's cheek, and dappled little kisses all the way back to her mouth. 'Let's go out on the deck,' I said.

'No, I can't,' she said. She was worried about her husband, who was alone in the room, three decks below. I pulled back and saw her pale blue eyes, set against her loose, weathered skin. I imagined her naked for a moment, the thinning skin, the calluses, the sunspots, the veins. 'What the hell am I doing,' I thought to myself. I was trying to seduce a 55 year-old to spite her daughter because she didn't seem to like me as much a I liked her.

Looking back, I still have no idea why I did any of it. It gives me chills, like someone's stuck a metal pole through the center of my spine. I wish I could erase the whole week from the ledger of my life, like meeting notes being swept from a whiteboard.

Instead, I'll just badmouth cruises every chance I get and, hopefully, will never set sail on one again.

Buying New Underwear, or Sex in a Dressing Room

I once went to a press event in downtown San Francisco. I spent the morning and part of the afternoon listening to media briefings, chatting with PR people, snapping photos, and trying to figure out what would be worth writing about. Just as the conference room lights and business-friendly chatter was making me feel trapped, like I was in a windowless nuclear bunker, I decided to get out. The first place I could think of escaping to was H&M, where I bought a bunch of new underwear to wash the business casual sterility out of my pants.

I didn't need more underwear at that point in my life. I had a drawer filled to the very top with intimate wear that could last three or four weeks without a washing. Underwear shopping was a new vanity I'd given in to. I still get excited for a few minutes every morning when I know I'll be putting on a colorful new pair of underpants. I stare at myself in the mirror for a few minutes before putting on my pants, taking in my body, the swells of cotton, the edge where the hem becomes skin.

A few years ago, I had the thought that my perfect sexual mate would be a clone of myself. I would know every last little corner of the body, and might feel some disembodied pleasure in sharing that knowledge with an intimate doppelganger. Is it gay if it's with yourself? Buying new underwear in the afternoon on a Wednesday is a concession to that metaphysical ghost, my shadow lover.

In that way, shopping has become vaguely sexual to me. The crowds of curious strangers, the idealized ensembles, the impersonal optimism of the music, the white walls and the collage of expressive colors framed in restrictive white box buildings. They want to lure you into the mirage of a better version of yourself, thinner, sleeker, and perfectly unique. Everyone mulls around in comparative silence searching for their own personal mirage.

N told me she had sex in a dressing room once. It's hard to describe the flames of jealousy that rose inside me when she told me this. I've never had sex in a dressing room, but I can't think of a single sexual experience I would want more than that. It must be such a startling experience to find yourself in a small boxed room in the heart of a department store, stripping down to your underwear, staring at yourself nearly naked in the mirror, anticipating the discovery of some new skin, a flattering pair of pants or a fitted shirt, and then instead begin fucking. To be in the cement bowels of Union Square, shivering under the heatless lights, and to be there with someone else. Swoon.

The next morning, I put on one of the pairs of underwear that I bought that day. They looked amazing on the rack, the color seemed like it would mesh perfectly with my skin tone under the store lights, the bright elastic band seemed like a perfect little to have poking above the belt line of my jeans. It seemed perfect imagining it there on the rack. The vision didn't survive the trip to my apartment, but I was stuck with it. And so I covered it with a pair of coarse, dark pants.

How to Pick Up a Bartender

One day I was sitting at a corner table in a bar watching a man with a laptop bag still around his shoulder hitting on the bartender. He was cute, curly black hair flecked with white, dressed in one layer too many for the weather. The bartender was thickish with a pretty face and small breasts mashed into a tight black top.

Everyone wants to sleep with the bartender. How could you not be attracted to a person who appears in dark and drunken light, half a body floating indifferently through the murk, looking you straight in the eye and asking you what you want? Even when they're not attractive, they're beautifully unaffected. There is nothing I could say to a bartender that hasn't been said already.

No pun, no insinuation of attraction, no trick of eye contact during an innocuous question. Bartenders are romantic Sibyls, obscure Tina Turners waiting for someone with a grin full of hope to step up and lie to them about how great things might be. They have nothing but time. This guy at the bar had been talking, making jokes, asking questions, putting on a show of being uninterested for more than half an hour. She smiled at him. She nodded in acknowledgement, walking back and forth to customers, washing glasses and working the beer spouts. She smiled, and gave nothing.

He finally paid his tab and left. 'Thanks for the hospitality,' he said, rising from the bar stool.

I tended bar one summer when I was 19, between my freshman and sophomore years at college. I got a job working in the tourist village in Yosemite. I lived in a tent cabin beside a parking lot, working split shifts all summer. 8AM until 2PM and then 5PM to Midnight. In the mornings I worked the cash register at the ice cream shop, and in the evenings I'd pour pitchers at the bar in the pizza parlor.

Most of the people I worked with were felons. At that time there was a recruitment program that offered employment in national parks to people recently released from prison. My roommate had just finished serving two years for beating another man with a tire iron. One of my neighbors had done five years for something relating to cocaine (he always demurred when I asked him for details). I cried while sitting on a log in the parking lot on my first day.

I spent the summer trying seduce H, a waitress in the pizza parlor. She was a puffy-lipped brat from Orange County. She was bony and talked about ska bands and surfing all the time. I would watch her from behind the bar gliding through the small circular tables in the manufactured lodge where we worked. When she returned to the bar with her orders I would steal details of her face; the little fissures in her lips, the translucent freckles across her round cheeks.

I found out she had a boyfriend my last day in camp. I got drunk with my neighbors, the felons. We drank Southern Comfort and goaded another boy who had gone to my high school and had a learning disability into wrestling a bear cub in the parking lot. I had the first hangover of my life the next day.

I used to watch the television show The Pick-Up Artist, in which a lanky man in a puffy fur hat said the best way to pick up a bartender is to feign indifference. Lean against the bar with your back towards her and avoid eye contact as much as possible. Condescension about her servile position is advisable. 'What do you have going for yourself besides looks?' he suggested to his pupils as an opening.

You can't pick up the bartender. The bartender doesn't exist. But if you keep your mouth shut and look them in the eye without flinching at the right time, they might want to pick up you. And the prize is waking up the next morning with someone completely new in bed next you. It might even be a felon.

The Funny Thing About Handjobs

I used to have a stupid habit. I would go into a social setting and wager some arbitrary sum of money that no one in the room could make me come in less than 10 minutes. I thought it was an innocuous icebreaker, but once somebody actually took me up on it.

I had forgotten the word 'handjob' existed until I saw Rushmore. There's a scene in which two 14-year-olds debate the claim that a mother is giving out handjobs in a local swimming pool. The idea of someone bragging about having their penis fondled is ridiculous. I wouldn't have singled it out anymore than I would have described the kind of mustard in the sandwich I ate for lunch today. There was definitely mustard in it, and it was an important part of the sandwich. But saying there was mustard does little to really describe the experience as a whole.

Hearing the debate about the sexual version of condiments was a small revelation for me. I had forgotten about the adolescent fixation on sex as achievement. Oh my god, this is great, I've got to hurry up and finish so I can tell my friends. The term handjob is so hairless and deliberate. It's perfectly juvenile to think of being in the same room with a woman and having done nothing more interesting than a manual pistoning of one's penis. It's something only a 14 year-old could marvel at, and I most definitely used to be that 14 year-old.

It amused me to walk into a room of comparative strangers soliciting a handjob with an ineptly transparent wager. To my thinking, it was a good way to loosen a stiff crowd and bend conversation toward territory that was more personal. I became the vulgar buffoon by going too far, but hopefully some people would feel a little bit less timid about taking conversational risks of their own.

Then one time, a friend of mine took me literally. I was trying to pass out on a couch after a party when my friend S coerced a woman into calling my bluff about the handjob bet. I heard some muffled conversation coming from outside and suddenly I felt a warm body lying on top of me. I felt someone's tongue licking my lips, and a hand worked its way into my pants. I had spent the evening drinking rum and snorting Phenobarbital (which was a bad idea).

I opened my eyes and recognized my friend L above me. We had hooked up once before so it made a little more sense that I was suddenly involved in foreplay when I had just wanted to go to sleep. But I knew what was happening and it was disconcerting to be called out about something so openly ridiculous.

I was in bad shape. I felt like the inside of a bar drain, grimy and sick. I liked L. She was smarter than me and wore glasses that darkened in the sun. I wasn't sure if I wanted to have sex with her, but I probably would have been convinced had I been in better shape.

Instead, I became the butt of my own joke. She couldn't make me come in less than 10 minutes. I couldn't even get an erection.

Thus ended my brief phase of making handjob jokes.

There's a Possibility You've Been Infected With HIV

One day I was standing in line at the sandwich counter in the small cafeteria by my office when my phone rang. It was my doctor. A week earlier I had blood drawn to check my T-Cell count and the results were abnormally low. My T-Cell count was 363 per microliter, healthy people have between 500 and 1500. My doctor spoke in a worried and irritated voice, he sounded like he didn't understand something and didn't want to say more than was necessary. 'There's a possibility you've been infected with the HIV virus,' he said. 'I'd like you to come down and get tested as soon as you can.'

This was the worst day I've ever had. Getting STD scares has become a relatively common experience. I remember talking to an older friend who marveled at how stressful it must be having sex in a world where HIV exists. He grew up in the sixties, a self-described sexual acrobat whose biggest concern was herpes and pregnancy. Having a potentially life-threatening consequence to sex was incomprehensible. I scoffed when he said this. Sex is no different than driving. No one marvels at how close to death they are when they merge onto a freeway. They buckle their seatbelts, turn their blinkers on, and check the rearview mirror.

When I hung up the phone, it seemed like I could feel the metal frame of a car crumpling in around me. I was dizzy and my head hurt. It felt like I had broken my nose against the dashboard in a bloom of shattering glass. This wasn't a guilt-ridden hunch about some Saturday night way back when, this was something tangible, a panicked doctor with a concrete figure on a lab sheet pointing toward HIV infection.

I spent the rest of the day in an andrenalized haze. My hands shook at the keyboard, I wrote without any understanding of the words I was stringing together. Questions started orbiting around in my head, trapped in some dark and nauseating gravity. Where could I have gotten HIV? Who should I tell? Could I have given it to anyone else? How do I tell my parents? How long can I live? What will my funeral be like? Am I going to wind up bankrupt paying for retroviral cocktails?

I looked at co-workers in the break room with a mix of greed and shame. I was suddenly envious of their normal, uninfected lives. I wanted to vomit every time someone said hello. I wanted to blurt it out into people's faces as I refilled my water bottle at this sink. 'How's it going?' they would ask. 'Well, it looks like I'm dying. I have HIV, if you're wondering what seems different about me today.'

I left work at 5:45 and immediately started calling friends, leaving a bunch of restrained messages about just wanting to say hello, got some kind of shitty news today so maybe when you get a chance give me a call back. My friend P was the first to call back. He walked me through all of the different things that could lead to a low T-Cell count; everything from leukemia to malnutrition and stress. My friend J, a licensed HIV counselor, explained how unlikely it was that HIV was the cause given that I had tested negative two months earlier after my last real exposure To have tested negative and then have the viral load increase so significantly that it could affect T-Cell counts in 6 weeks was highly unlikely.

As comforting as it was, I couldn't let go of the idea that I could be infected. Probabilities work for other people, but it was too much to assume everything was going to be okay based on some statistics that I was barely lucid enough to grasp. When the doctor called, it felt like my life slipped right out of my hands and hung suspended in the distance between me and some future moment where my results would be disseminated. Positive. Negative.

I had blood drawn the next morning. I went into work late. I had a slight fever and chills from the sudden rush of anxiety, my eyes were dry and irritated. I kept imagining telling my parents that they would outlive me. I imagined my friends at 50, living without me. I imagined the end: weak, struggling with barely contained illnesses, bedridden, broke, in some antiseptic hospital bed holding my mother's hand, unable to blow out the lone candle on my 40th birthday cupcake.

I decided not to tell my parents until I got the results. There were some people I could be vulnerable with, and some people I felt obligated to. I would not fall apart to my parents. That night my dad was coming through the city. He was going to a conference in the morning and was going to spend the night at my apartment. He picked me up from work and we drove back into the city together, chatting about work, movies, politics. We went out for Vietnamese food. I asked him how his noodles were five times over the course of dinner. When the check came I opened my fortune cookie. It said I should write to an old friend I haven't spoken to in years. My stomach dropped, I looked at the floor wrestling off another wave of adrenaline. Even the fortune cookie seemed to understand that my premature death was imminent.

We walked the five blocks back to my apartment and I pulled out the guest mattress. My dad had been up early and his head was nodding down in sleep every few minutes sitting on the couch. I have a studio apartment so there was no point staying up if he was ready for bed, and I was exhausted. The night before I had tossed and turned, sweating through awful death and sex dreams. Going to sleep with my dad in the same room was a small relief. It reminded me of being a kid and nosing into my parents' bed some night when I was too scared to fall asleep. Even as a grown man there was some superstitious lure to having a parent asleep a few feet away that made every overwhelming thought seem manageable. The night before I felt like I was alone and drowning. With my dad there, I felt safe, afloat in a boat, under stars, nearing some new shore.

Then I got my results back. I was HIV negative.

Let's Make Babies

When I was in my mid-20s I decided that I would adopt a child when I turned 32. I didn't. At 32 I lived in a one-room studio and had just quit my job to move across the country. I was nowhere near stable enough to convince any adoption agency that I would be parenting material. I don't imagine being able to settle down in either respect over the next several years, and I think I can feel the beginnings of all my dead babies drying up inside me.

I'm not even sure if I want kids. When I was younger, having children was just another unspoken expectation. It was hard to imagine a life for myself that didn't involve mirroring the patterns of my parents. When the time came I would get a job which required a briefcase, then I would settle down and marry someone who looks good in a picture frame. I wanted kids in the same way a lot of 8-year-olds want to be doctors, because they're told to want it.

After I graduated from college and had spent a few years working I began to have some extended conversations with my metaphysical self during all those lost moments (staring idly at a red light in rush hour on a Tuesday) that eventually turn into the shape of our lives. 'Why am I here?' I asked the stoplight at Pico and La Cienega. Was I meant to be a script reader for a warship talent agency, to one day be able to say that my comments helped shape a Ben Stiller comedy that opened number three at the box office in some distant March?

I decided the truth must be to propagate the world for generations to come with offspring willing to carry my wisdom forward. I imagined having a child would be an opportunity to take all the things I've done right with my life and make them even better. Beneath that, I wanted to hold a baby in my arms. Behind all the fancy rhetoric and strung out syllables, the drive to hold a child was really what I felt sitting in traffic.

It's easy to romanticize the idea of having children, especially with all the patriarchal weight of culture and tradition. The strength of that romantic ideal can push people in a relationship to get even closer, especially after a certain age. Once the uterus starts sending out hormonal smoke signals, the push to just find someone so that they can move forward into the childbearing sorority is powerful. A friend described that phenomenon to me one night in a long conversational meander. The guy's good enough, but the real prize is the crib and the country home.

I've never understood why men don't express more of the romantic side of having a family. Men seem to accumulate wife, child, and house as accessories. One of my friends still evaluates women like suits, determining their worth based on how well he can imagine them at his family Christmases and office picnics. It's as if getting a stable wife would be the last criterion for total victory over life.

I could tell an adoption agency that I'd like to raise a child to pass on the love and wisdom that I've collected over the years, to help contribute something positive into the world. I could say that raising a well-educated and financially stable child would be the ultimate validation of my life choices, freeing me to gloat from the porch in retirement. But the truth is that I just want to hold a baby in my arms.

Maybe I should get a terrier instead. I would if I had been willing to pay the extra $300 deposit for pet owners that my landlord requires. Don't tell the adoption agency.

The Three-Year Itch

How long can you stay in a relationship? Two years? Three years? Ten, maybe? I'm terrible at long-term relationships. I've never been in one that lasted more than a year, all things considered; and even then that period has been spiked with turbulence and uncertainty.

My friend B told me she starts to feel restless sometime during the third year of a relationship. That seems like a fair amount of time, right when the thrill of discovery wears off. After the rush of falling in love and the secret thrill of shared intimacy, the third year of a relationship leaves you with a simple human being not a bundle of metaphysical promises. The great universal answer to our search for love becomes a stupefying anti-climax, a moment when the love adrenaline wears off and the weight of the yoke starts to make your neck sore.

Realizing a relationship is going to require work and patience isn't such a terrible thing, but the three-year marker is when many people figure out just how much effort that can mean. It's when you realize the really hard stuff is yet to come. So it's natural to ask if you really want to put yourself through all that for the person you're with. The answer is 'no' more often than we like to admit.

Of course this is all conjecture, since I don't have any direct personal experience to reference. I've never gone that long because I've never found someone I knew in advance I'd want to fight for, and who also wanted to fight for me. I get nervous when I'm dating someone and I don't feel my metaphysical babies tingling in the ether. I fall in love easily, and hard. Being with someone and knowing I'm not in love with them makes me deeply uncomfortable. I worry that I'm pulling some sham on them.

But then, what begins as ambivalence and unassuming fun

can just as quickly become fond familiarity. In the absence of other options, and not having any particular motivation to seek out new ones, a simple fling can turn into piece of luggage; a burden that's cumbersome but filled with caring nostalgia, if not passionate love. I went through this with one of my first girlfriends. We started seeing each other in the summer. We hooked up lots, laughed together, and teased each other. There wasn't any thought of a relationship in my head. I didn't really understand what was happening, but I didn't stop to think about it.

Until I stopped to think about it. It had been three months and things were changing. It felt like the teeth in some universal gear had been moving all along, but only now was it becoming apparent. The improvised fun was becoming predictable. The jokes were starting to ring hollow, picking up hard edges that hadn't been there before. I wanted a relationship, but I thought that was something that inevitably happened. I didn't realize it was a choice you have to make; to look someone in the eye and agree to stay with that person to the exclusion of all other romance.

I started to think about whether or not this was the person I wanted to be in a relationship with. The accumulated weight of those brief few months started to build into a looming expectation. I started to wonder if I wanted to commit further to a person who I had never had a serious conversation with, whose teasing felt like it was turning into bickering. I didn't want it. She seemed hurt. She said she didn't understand why we couldn't just keep having fun together the way we had been.

We could have. But I kept thinking about all the things I would have to close a door on to do that. I didn't want to close that door and be left with only her. So I left.

Why Women Suck in Bed

Performance anxiety is usually something attributed to men. We are expected to get hard in an instant, hold out for an hour, understand the nuances of how the clitoris, labia, g-spot, and vaginal walls all work in unison, then keep them happily moving forward towards orgasm land. On top of all that we're supposed to have thick eight-inchers capable of running deep and wide. A lot of men take pleasure in bragging about their competitive capacities, either in terms of wang size or proficiency at making vaginas gush nectar. Trying to manage all of those complex operations while subconsciously wondering just how their performance ranks in terms of skill and general 'good'-ness can be enough to kill a boner before it's even out of a man's pants.

I don't know whether or not this phenomenon of performance anxiety exists for women. I don't have a comprehensive body of knowledge from which to draw, but my anecdotal evidence has led me to the conclusion that most straight women are lousy lays. If there are strict requirements of skill to accompany the acts of lapping a woman's mucus flaps, there must be an equally complex and demanding list of instructions for how to handle a penis.

For many women, it seems like the simple act of touching a penis should be an earth-shaking event, or at least a favor bestowed. Once contact is made, the only remaining need is to monotonously jack the beast back and forth until the skies open up and the man turns into a quivering mess for 30 seconds. One woman I hooked up with reminded me of this fact. After grabbing my penis while we were kissing in bed, I let out an encouraging moan. Apparently this was the signal to go for broke as she instantly switched into fifth gear and started pistoning away as if I was seconds from coming, and without any lubrication.

Blowjobs also seem to be some unspoken gift that should make a man crumble in ecstasy. The sheer fact that a woman is willing to put her head in between a man's legs should be enough to guarantee a week's worth of gratitude. I almost never come from head. If you can imagine the act of repetitively licking away at the clit (or offering up the dread back-and-forth headwag), then transpose that to the penis and you'll get a fair comparison. Just because there are lot of nerve endings on the penis doesn't mean that variation, sensitivity, and multiple points of stimulation at differing times and different intensities aren't required to really make the act more pleasurable than a warm mouth-bath. A stunning majority of the blowjobs I've ever gotten tend towards the nob-slobbering, up-and-down variety with a ball tickle or a finger in the ass if the woman's feeling extra self-assured. It's not that having a mouth go up and down over a penis feels bad; it's nice. But it gets boring quickly.

Many of the women I've been with approach sex with was an unspoken passivity, as if the thrill of being desired and sought after is the most exciting part. When some women finally accept a suitor they can become supine and indulgent.

I'm protesting too much, taking a bunch of random encounters that didn't turn into relationships to validate a general argument. Still, I see a connection between the way women are born and bred to be constantly pursued, to need the man to be the first one to call, to not make the first move, to call their peers sluts for being sexually aggressive; and the larger experiences I've had with women who are lousy in bed.

Our culture celebrates the art of the hook-up and the 'great fuck.' We believe in concepts like being 'good in bed,' but how can you be good in bed if you look at a clump of nerve endings as the secret answer to anything? Jack them, lick them, suck them, bite them, take them inside. The secret of great sex is realizing that those nerve endings are attached to an entire body filled with nerve endings, and those nerve endings report directly back to the brain, which tells the heart to beat and the blood to flow. In truth, there are no rules to being good or bad in bed. You only have to listen, and experiment, and adapt. Yet it very often seems we've stubbornly kept women propped up on the plinth of history and culture, turning them into a metaphysical acquisition, of which the possessing is enough.

I Kissed A Boy

I was 25 the first time I kissed another man. It wasn't a playful peck or some ironic beso, this was an open-mouthed salivary exchange. It was during a game of spin the bottle so it wasn't exactly arousing, but I remember it very clearly. I thought kissing a male mouth would feel like a cross between a garbage disposal and beef jerky. In the world of the sports-consuming, beer-guzzling straight man, the concept of sexualizing another man is a revolting threat. ESPN fans talk about women with the same fixated affection that they reserve for fine cuts of steak. The tales of their sexual exploits sound like a pre-historic hunting yarn that culminates in some blushing attempt at bravura. 'Let's just say she had a good time,' you might overhear from the next table at a Hooters on game day. As I was moving in for the final approach to kiss this man, I felt apprehension and a flickering revolt. 'This is going to be gross,' I thought.

I was in high school when I started wondering what it was that separated men and women on a chemical level. I was convinced that the molecular composition of a man's mouth had to be entirely different from that of a woman's. It seemed like an inherent certainty, but I couldn't understand how or why. I imagined doing a kissing test, taking ten mouths and pushing them through some scientifically approved glory hole. How accurately could someone guess the gender based on taste alone? I remember pulling out my lower lip and looking at the shiny inner edge in the bathroom mirror one day. How can this be any different from a woman's inner lip?

When I finally kissed R it was a giant anti-climax. His mouth was wet, warm, and smooth, just like anyone else's. His saliva tasted neutral, almost flavorless. It wasn't putrid, nauseating, or filthy. It was just boring. My tongue swished around inside his mouth in disbelief. I thought I was missing something. I thought there must be some oral g-spot in there that releases a flood of musky pheromones. I couldn't believe there wasn't some physical trigger that made the process nauseating. Shouldn't this taste at least as bad as when my old dog would come around and slobber on my face?

It made me think of a night a few years earlier, when I had gone skinny dipping with a few friends. After running around in the middle of the night, naked, breaking into a public pool, and baiting some hapless security guard on a wild goose chase, my friend and I tried to convince the two women we were with to kiss each other. The woman I had been seeing relented and they shared a short, closed-mouth kiss. This was just enough to draw cruel jeers from my friend and me. There should be no half-measures. We demanded a full-on lesbian exchange.

I felt bad about putting so much pressure on them. I didn't really care whether or not they kissed. I was pretty sure that watching them kiss wouldn't turn me on at all, and I didn't want to push the woman I was seeing into doing something she didn't want to do.

I've never understood the way straight men fetishize lesbianism while turning a scornful eye to man-on-man expressions of affection. When it's born of genuine attraction it just adds a layer of distance. I can't imagine there being a place for me in between two women already having sex. When it's the product of social pressure to show off, or comes from the impulse perform for the hooting hordes of football fans licking hot wings sauce from their fingers, it's even more dispiriting. It's never possible to underestimate what people will put themselves through for attention and a sense of acceptance.

I used to torture my male friends with the fact that I had kissed other men before. I would needle them with it over and over again, watching their faces turn from unresponsive to antagonistic in a few seconds. I enjoyed the act because it was vulgar, separating the action of a kiss from its deeper purpose of attraction. It was as much fun as telling a handjob joke at a black tie function. One new year's eve I was in Texas and gave a friend a short little lip licking in a bar to celebrate the ball drop. I heard a woman who had been watching us say, 'That was so hot.' I immediately felt feminized and attractive, like some insecure freshman on a beach in front of a sea of men hooting and cheering. 'If that's the reaction I get, then bombs away,' I thought. All while the person I would have really wanted to kiss stood idly by with a beer in her hand, watching the show.

Picking Up Women in Gay Bars

According to guy lore, gay bars are the easiest places for a straight man to meet a woman. I remember casting the first short film I directed several years ago. I posted ads in Backstage West and met with dozens of actors after-hours in my boss's Beverly Hills office. One actor I spoke with quickly jumped from telling stories about his acting background into tales of sexual prowess. Hey look, ma! Somebody fucked me! Can you believe it?

This man swore that he could have sex with any woman in a gay bar. Their defenses are down, they feel safe, they vamp suggestively without having to worry that some guy is going to get the wrong idea, and they tend to drink heavily, chugging fruity two-for-one specials.

I had originally planned on shooting the short as an all-nude production. When I mentioned this to they actor he immediately stood up from his chair. 'I'll strip right now, if you want,' he said. 'I'm not ashamed of my body at all. You want me to get all the way naked?'

I've always had mixed feelings about gay bars. I don't like the idea of separating social groups based on sexual preference. Bars are bars. People get drunk, they dance, they try and meet someone new, many wind up bringing someone home later on. You're a little less likely to hear Tom Petty or Dire Straights in a gay bar, but otherwise, the idea is basically the same.

On the other hand, the gay bars I've been to have felt less serious and weighted down with social posturing than other straight bars. Would that there were more straight bars with porno playing on the walls.

The first gay bar I remember going to was in Austin. It was a lesbian night at a place called Boyz Cellar. All the bartenders were topless and covered in bodypaint. It was surreal to be in a room filled with women and not a single one paying attention to me. Knowing in advance that everyone in the bar was outside of my sexual purview took a lot of tension out of the air. I felt like I could stroll around leisurely and talk to anybody about anything. There was no worry about having intentions misconstrued or being shot down by a cranky diva.

After a couple of hours one of the friends I was with reached a level of dramatic intoxication and decided she needed to vomit in the corner. The bar manager saw her and asked that she leave. She was still lucid enough to feel insulted by this and went nose-to-nose with the pasty man for a few minutes before finally relenting.

I don't like the idea of having to pick someone up, no matter what the context. There has been a lot said for the thrill of the chase and wanting the unattainable, but I don't see the value in either. I don't believe in unattainability. We're all born out of the same primordial question mark. We all want to believe in someone. We are all attainable.

Chasing after someone is equally uninteresting. Why should I have to pursue someone who resists the idea of my companionship? If they don't want to spend time with me, what does it benefit me to convince them otherwise? I want to fight for the people who'll fight for me, and not chase after a trophy to validate my sense of achievement.

Those two ideas hang heavy in straight bars, like wooly fogs across the neon light. It might be easier to pick someone up in a gay bar. But it isn't any easier to fall in love.

Why Women Are Great in Bed

I remember H, the first woman who ever swallowed my come. I'm sure the blowjob itself was fantastically skillful and measured, but I don't remember anything in particular about it. What I do remember is she still had my penis in her mouth after I had finished, almost as if she wanted to make sure to get the most out of my fleshy little sprinkler head.

As she came back up and nestled into the crook of my armpit and ran her hands across my chest, I was completely swept away. I had only experienced swallowing in porn before, where the context is one of male domination and bukkake-tinted victory over another cock-hungry slut. Experienced in reality, I suddenly felt the meaning was completely the opposite. My girlfriend had found a physical language to express how much she cared about me and how much she was attracted to me. It was direct and selfless. I want you this much, it said. I love you this much. Only a woman could be so comfortable with the language of intimacy. I never would have asked her to swallow my come, I would have thought it a demeaning sleight because that's the only way I could imagine it in my narrow little brain. Where I might have been busy worrying about technique or performance issues to validate myself, she was focused entirely on me and seemed to have let go of her self completely.

Many of the women I've been with have been impulsive creatures whereas I'm always calculating and reserved. I think back on the modest list of public places that I've had sex (a park, the beach, a disco, stairwells ...) and I realize that none of it would have happened without my partners instigating things. I've come to have a great desire for sex in public over the years, but it's something I would have never had the courage to do when I was younger, not without some prompting from my adventuresome girlfriend at the time. There's a timidity I have about any kind of sex act in public, which probably stems from some latent fear of showing my little wee wee to everyone and then being judged by it. Likewise, there's probably plenty of anxiety about having my tricks and techniques judged by random strangers; kind of a waking version of the dream of arriving at school naked.

Every time I see people engaged in public sex it's always crude and garish, with sloppy groping and jaws looking as if they're trying to detach from the joint to wholly engorge the other person. I would have been mortified, as a young man, to let myself be so publicly vulnerable and oblivious to my own self-image. But then a soft-eyed woman with warm hands and a round belly pulled me into a booth in a disco and taught me how stupid it is to care. Sex is about you and me, she said with her mouth and hips and hands. It's not about how your sexual exploits make you seem to other people, it's about what you share with the person you're with at the time. Being impulsive is, among other things, a recognition that you don't have to apologize for who you are; it's the strength to be curious about what following one's native impulses and seeing what kinds of adventures come from them. It's something I would never have understood without the sex of a woman.

Then there's the matter of anatomy. I know well my previous use of the phrase 'mucus flaps' to describe the labia is potentially offensive. It's a blunt phrase, I confess, but no less accurate or pejorative than the word 'pussy,' 'beaver,' or 'nonny.' What it lacks in round-edged, kid-friendly vagueness, it makes up for in absurdity. I suppose it's the 'mucus' part which is most offensive, but I don't see how this is a pejorative at all. One of the surest indicators of how attracted I am to a woman is whether or not I start fantasizing about tasting her vaginal fluids. How many men haven't walked around the day after sex with the secret scent of vagina on their fingers, chin, or penis? To some the phrase 'mucus flaps' might induce revolt or socio-sexual indignation. To me it induces hunger, lust. Mmmmmucus.

If sex is an act that requires honesty and shameless communication with your partner, than our bodily excretions during it are the physical embodiment of all those embarrassing anxieties. There's nothing I like better than to have sex with a woman on her period. Our culture teaches us to fear vaginal odor and uterine sloughing. I've never smelled a fish in a vagina (and I've lapped vaginosis, remember), nor have I ever gotten squeamish about seeing blood and mucus during period sex. As a friend once described the beautiful fecundity to a vagina on its period. It's the scent of earth, and fertility, and the body calling out for sex. I've never felt fingers pull at my hair and claw at my back with the same urgency or need as when having sex with a woman on her period.

But for all the contraptions, acrobatics, geometry, and craven animal-sex of the most ambitious lovers I've ever had, the best sex I ever had remains the tamest. Laying in bed, holding her face between my hands, feeling every last ridge and flexing ripple of her mucus tunnel (is that any worse than 'love canal?'), kissing softly, slowly lapping her saliva into my mouth, looking into her dilated pupils. I'd give you back every other woman I've ever had sex with, a hundred times over, for 12 hours of that straight, boring, vanilla sex. I don't give a shit about technique at the end of the day. Lovers aren't like cleaning ladies, who you hire and fire based on skill, proficiency, or recommendation. They're people you communicate with, someone that you have something to say to in a language that only your body can articulate. I never would have known that so immediately without the impulsive, fearless, and shamelessly fecund love of a woman.

My Mother

After N left I started using the phrase 'love of my life.' It had never occurred to me to say it before. I had been in love plenty, and at various points felt like I would have been ready to make a life-long commitment to those different women. Still, I never would have thought to say one or the other was the love of my life. It's an ugly phrase, written on drug store cards, said in shabby television shows for very special episodes, and scrawled into high school diaries with dizzy abandon. I'm sure I don't know myself well enough to speak for what will happen next. I can't predict where I'll be in the next few years, so how could I expect to honestly say I know how I'll feel? How could I come to such a conclusory statement, speaking for an entire lifetime?

Parents allegedly form the romantic model that we're bound to pursue in our lives. Some people want to replicate mommy or daddy to continue the peaceful domesticity of their childhoods. Others fall in obstinate love with their parent's opposite as an extension of developmental anger and personal autonomy; to reject the unhappy models of their upbringing.

I was wholly in love with my mother when as a child. I swooned over her, found her scent in clothing and furniture, clung to her indulgently, romanticized her into soap operas so that all the faceless actresses in tight clothes and red lipsticks became ciphers for her.

I think I was 12 the first time I told her I hated her. I was trying to impress on her the fact that I needed to be driven across town to a friend's house and spend the night there. She was sitting in bed reading the paper and barely paying attention to me. I don't remember her reasoning, but she stood firm. I wouldn't be going. I felt betrayed. How could this woman stand in the way of my momentary happiness to such an unreasonable degree? I needed fun and play, exotic foods from the pantry of my friend's house, the luxury of his unfamiliar toys and videogames.

Instead I was shackled with the tedium of my own room and my own things. I could feel tears coming on the more I thought about it. I remember spitting out the words in a last gasp of brinksmanship to show how painfully serious my need was. I stormed out and sat on the floor of my room feeling spurned and abandoned. My dad followed me in and tried to mediate, explaining her position in some rational terms that I didn't pay attention to.

When I was in high school I fought with my mom like an entrenched solider. My parents' marriage was failing and she hammered against my father, bending every personal short-coming into a metaphor for how he had stopped caring. As this was happening, I followed right behind, bending back the responsibility for their onset fighting so that it pointed at her. She was the one picking all the fights, creating all the conflict.

When I was 17 I saw my mother cry for the first time in my life. I was driving around with her one gray afternoon, running errands when she started talking about why we had started to fight all the time. She started explaining her side of things, the sense of isolation and of not having a partner who cared about her. I pounced on the rhetorical opening, describing at length what a faithless and selfish partner she had been to my father.

Those arguments were rote by that point, they were thoughts I had let fly at her before. They always seemed to bounce off her impenetrable hull like foam pellets, becoming less and less impactful the harder I tried to hurl them.

This is the part where I want to stop writing; where the memory starts to taste like battery acid, and becomes shameful.

When I was finished talking, I saw her face soften in a way I hadn't seen before. We were stopped at a red light on Shaw and Palm in Fresno, CA. She was staring straight ahead at the stopped traffic in front of us. 'It would just be nice to know that someone was thinking about how I feel,' she said. Her face pulled against itself, something cracked in her cheek muscles. Her eyes looked wet and I saw the first line of a tear fall down her cheek, like the trace of a small finger.

When you fall in love with someone for the first time, you get swept away on a wave of your own emotion. It feels like you're being filled with thoughts and feelings that weren't there before. It animates you and it's something you can see in someone else. It's like being doped together. You feel the warm high spread through your body and your thoughts, and when you look beside you and see the same glazed over look on your lover's face, it feels like you've arrived. Watching my mother cry at a red light, knowing that it was because of something I had done, I felt like I was at the far end of that narcotic tunnel.

When the dim shape of those words, 'love of my life' began taking shape in my head, it wasn't on the upslope of some ambrosial high. It wasn't the gauzy idealism of looking at a new lover and feeling surprise at having wound up with them. If there's one thing you learn from parents it's that you can't ever walk away from them. You can cut them off, stop talking to them, tuck them away into a mental lockbox and pretend they don't exist. But they're always there, the whispering voice you hear when you're alone and defenseless.

I was later in the hospital with my mother. We would walk laps around the 5th floor as part of her recovery routine. In one room we kept passing, a woman with white hair was lying flat on her back. She was crying out someone's name, over and over again. 'Ben! Beeeen!' She would arch her hips upwards and push her chin toward the ceiling with each call. She sounded like she was in trouble, had fallen, and wouldn't be able to rise again on her own.

The love of your life: the person you miss most when there's nothing else left.

Sex With 19-Year-Olds

I was waiting for the BART after work in San Francisco on day when I noticed a nervous-looking woman glancing at me out of the corner of her eye. She had bleached-blonde hair, cut short and scruffy like a boy's. She was in tight black jeans and black eyeliner, meandering up and down the platform chewing on her lower lip. When she would come closest to me we'd look at each other for a second, then she would turn around. Then she'd come back and we'd catch each other staring again. I was about to talk to her when I looked closer and realized she was much younger than I had thought, probably 19 at the oldest.

It's strange for me to think of age as a barrier to attraction, but it is. Men are supposed to want delicate young things as some vestigial proof of their virility. Quelling a trembling fawn of a young woman with an assured stroke must be the very embodiment of all that is manly, macho, and authoritative.

It's hard to understand what aging really is. I remember one summer I spent a week in a cabin with a friend and his parents. I was 12. I remember sneaking out to the porch one night and looking out at the dark trees and impenetrable blackness beneath them. The air was just cold enough to excite the bare skin on my arms. I looked up at the stars and felt a vast sameness inside. It felt just as I felt when I was a small boy, totally unchanged inside.

I still feel that same way now, more than 20 years later. I have all the same questions I had before, the same excitements, the same longings, the same contentment in just being alive.

But I am older. I look older, my speech is more convoluted, my thoughts riddled with a gypsy trove of collected facts to support my hunches and metaphysics. When I look back on pictures of my 19-year-old self it's hard to not feel stunned at how different I was. If I felt the same then as now, why did I wear those strange expressions, have that embarrassed posture, wear those terrible clothes designed to make me a part of the unnoticed background?

Looking at the young girl giving me moon eyes on the BART platform, I felt a flush of ego. If I talked to her, bummed a cigarette, snuck her into some skanky dive bar, walked around the dirty cement corridors of the city letting her exorcise her nervous stories of anxiety and disbelief, we would eventually have sex. If that happened, my inner caveman would surely sprout a new chest hair.

I went out with a woman several years younger than me a while back (I was 29, she was 22). We went dancing. Or more precisely, she tried to teach me how to dance, offering to show me what to do before we had even stepped on the dance floor. She had a kind of mania, filled with nerves and bravura, confident in the fact that there was a right way to do something as personal as dancing. Being with her that night was exhausting, it was like having fun by algebra or assimilation to some social standard that finally amounted to her bouncing around on the balls of her feet to a 4/4 beat. Later, headed back to my apartment she assured me that she was going to blow my mind in bed because she was bisexual.

When I was younger, I felt like I had something to apologize for, but I wasn't sure what. I always felt like I was the one puzzle piece that was out of place. I overcompensated by trying to appear impenetrable. I tried to control my vulnerability and embarrassment by projecting it on other people. I believed there was a right way and a wrong way to do something, to dance, to talk to a woman, to wear some article of clothing.

When I think of having sex with someone so young now, all I can see is my own cagey self, full of mania and a constant fear of being discovered as a fraud. I would have kissed like a blender and had sex like a broken spring. When the BART Train pulled up I watched the young girl get into the last car on the train. I thought about following her for a second. Instead, I went into the car ahead of hers and put on my headphones. I tried to remember all those things I've always felt while the metal roar of the tracks shook the whole train around me.

The Gun Show, or Is That All You Got?

I went out with a woman one night, and while we were walking to a bar for drinks she grabbed my arm and asked me to flex. I held my arm out for her and she squeezed the modest swells underneath my sweater. 'Is that it?' she asked. A submerged part of my ego winced. It's hard to imagine a romantic scenario in which hearing those words can count as a good thing.

'Yeah,' I told her. 'That's it.' It's true. I don't have big muscles. I've always been lanky, and that's especially true now. I felt inadequate for a split second, like I was failing to live up to an unspoken expectation that I have strapping muscles and chest hair. Men aren't supposed to be bony and pale, we're supposed to be fleshy monuments of stability, comfort, and permanence. Macho.

After I got over the initial surprise of having my physique called out, I found that I enjoyed the candor of being able to say whatever I wanted in return. Going on a date can become so weighted down with manners, wanting to behave your best to make sure the other person likes you. Even when I know I'm not interested in the other person I still feel the tug of propriety. I don't want to be blunt or hurt someone's feelings. So I fake it to make things nice.

But we all have interior monologues running all the time. There's nothing to apologize for with my body, though I'm certain there are plenty of people in the world who wouldn't be attracted to it. I wasn't expecting my date to be one of those people, especially considering this was our second time out.

I like my body. Whatever I do in this world begins and ends with it. It contains the root of everything I'll ever be. It's my alphabet. It doesn't resemble a lot of the male iconography in the media. It doesn't look like a movie star or an athlete. There might have been an analog in a sitcom, a bit player who wandered into a scene who briefly stole the limelight with a spindly assemblage of knees and shoulder blades.

I stare at my body in the mirror almost every day, sometimes several times. It always surprises me. It looks so different throughout the days and weeks, sometimes gaunt and sucked in, other times soft and swollen. Some days it's pale and splotchy, other days it's relaxed and flushed with color. Social conventions encourage us to feel shame, but of all the experiences I have when I look on my body alone, embarrassment is entirely absent.

It's the introduction of someone else's gaze that inspires those feelings. There's an impulse to commodify yourself, to be desirable, to feel the dislocated pleasure of becoming an object in someone else's eyes. That desire can become quantified, reduced into a hazy distillation of self-worth. It's a way of putting the burden down for a few moments, to let the weight of your own body be buoyed up by the admiring look of someone down below.

My date asked me to flex while she was squeezing my bicep. She wanted to see if there wasn't some hidden muscle waiting to magically inflate itself on command. I told her no.

Living Like A Bachelor

When I moved to New York I shared an apartment with two women after living alone for more than a year. Going through the process made me realize how low my standards for food and neatness and neatness had been.

When I'm seeing someone it's much easier to set aside time and energy to think about what to have for dinner or making time to relax at the end of the day. I love food and am especially fixated on cooking. I look forward to the nights when I have to grocery shop and have no idea what to buy. Wandering around the aisles thinking about what might be created from everything waiting on the shelves has always been a secret pleasure. Doing it with someone else, or just knowing that improvised planning will be for a fond someone adds to the allure.

Going out to dinner is its own separate sport. Choosing a kind of food to settle on for the evening is like picking out what kind of clothes to wear in the morning. You can rush through it, or spend an inordinate amount of time trying to conceive the perfect mix of function and newness. 'What do you feel like?' we ask each other.

When I'm on my own, all that thought disappears. Food becomes one of the lowest priorities in my list of daily necessities. The first day in my new place I realized what a dope I looked like sitting down on a Sunday night with a dinner of potato chips and a couple of quartered and salted tomatoes.

When I don't have to think about anyone else, my ability to feed myself is stripped down to pure functionality. When I lived in Los Angeles I went through an extended phase of eating canned beans and spaghetti sauce for dinner. Perhaps it's a sign of gradual sophistication that I've now moved onto canned beans sautéed with onions and dumped onto couscous. This is a slightly more elaborate variation, but it can be prepared mindlessly and repeatedly.

It's ugly though. One of my roommates compared this concoction to pig slop one night.

My standards for neatness are also remarkably low. I'm more than capable of leaving dishes in the sink for a whole week, and my hamper is usually a Vesuvial overflow of socks and underwear. I've never clocked how long I could go without changing my bed sheets, but I know it's a long time.

My only real defense for this slovenliness is that I work a lot. When I'm with someone, I am content. All those pressing needs about career and expansion turn into appreciation for all the small moments in between; an evening spent thinking up something new to do with a mushroom, or sitting together on the couch listening to a record and talking.

These are all moments that could just as easily be enjoyed alone, or with a friend. But I am loath to let myself indulge in them at the end of the day when I am on my own. I do sometimes, but those times are rare.

When you're young and have no idea what to do, you lean on people for guidance and perspective, a gentle push in the right direction. The older you get the more you realize no one can finally make those choices for you; we all have to become our own essential critics. This is the one true mark of a bachelor, a willingness to undergo sloth and filth for the sake of a life lived with a party ball and an interesting CV.

Because I Can

I was out one weekend just after moving to New York and a woman asked me to come home with her. There's a theory that scarcity makes sex more desirable. The harder a person is to attain the more we yearn to possess them. We catch glimpses of what their sex might be like; the smell of warm skin on the first hot night of the year, the darkening shadow in the space between the breast and bra, the teasing line said without thought for the strained urges it might inspire.

I don't believe in it. Finding someone you're attracted to feels good, but it doesn't make you a better person. I tend to lose interest in people when they present themselves as unattainable. (That line probably elicits groans from a few friends who, having followed along the underbelly of my romantic life for the last few years, would argue that the opposite is true.)

Conspicuous consumption has become intuition for many of us. I grew up watching my brother feed his belts through the label on his jeans so that everyone could see he was wearing Calvin Kleins. Value is created on the supply side. We can be made to want something because the label tells us it's scarce and worth wanting. Few could tell the difference in the fabric, threading, cut, and dye, but we let the label assure us that the jeans are worth $150. It's an act of faith or self-perpetuating intuition.

In the same way, an unattractive man in a shabby suit might suddenly become intriguing if he walks into a bar with a beautiful woman. Or the woman might become dramatically more desirable because of make-up, body type, or a style of dress that mimics something upwardly mobile. We want people to believe we're better than them to bait their pursuit, which blots out our own insecurities for a moment or two.

But so there I was, drunk and talking to a woman running her index finger along the small of my back, suggesting I crash at her place instead of trudging 30 blocks uptown. I knew from the minute I saw her that I didn't want to sleep with her. She was pretty, had a nice body, and was personable. I also felt that our personalities were at loggerheads. There was no sexual grist, no foreboding. Like her sense of humor, everything about her seemed earnest and deliberate. We would have bad physical chemistry.

She could have been as aloof and unattainable as she pleased, I wouldn't have felt any greater need to be with her.

When the proposition came I had to reconsider everything. The fact that she was so forthright and deliberate about stating what she wanted made her more attractive. Her attainability was an aphrodisiac. I didn't feel any more or less attracted to her physically, but I felt more willing to take a gamble. I didn't especially want her but knowing that she wanted me made me wonder if I hadn't overlooked something. For a few minutes I was more attracted to her than I would otherwise have been.

I didn't go home with her. It was late, I was tired, I felt nauseous from too much booze, and I knew, from past experience, that things generally go poorly when I jump into sex with someone without an animal yearning. But I was dangling by a thread for a few minutes, a sex deer in the come-on headlights.

My Kingdom for a Boner

A woman I once knew confessed that almost every man she had slept with over the age of 35 had some form of erectile dysfunction. Either they would get hard and then go limp a few minutes later, take 20 minutes or more to get erect from direct stimulation, or just never get hard at all. I've heard the Viagra jokes, seen the Bob Dole commercials, seen the sitcom one-liners about it happening to everyone, but was still surprised to hear that this tacky bit of cultural floss actually has a kernel of truth in it.

I remember the first time I couldn't get an erection with a woman. I was 25. We had been kissing for a couple of hours one sweltering August afternoon. It was with a woman I had been dating for a few weeks but hadn't had sex with yet. 'Do you want to put something in me besides your fingers?' she asked. Yeppers.

We made our way to her bed. She was naked and I was in an ugly pair of plaid boxer shorts. I watched her walk to a dresser across the room to get condoms. It was 90 degrees inside and humid. We had been out late the night before, drinking and dancing. I still had a hangover and I felt the achy tickle of a cold coming on. As soon as she left the bed, I felt a strange reaction in my body. It felt tired, like a mule after a long haul. The distraction of fooling around and the immediate touch of another body had been enough to cover it up, but now that she was on the other side of bedroom, rooting through her sock drawer, there were no distractions left. I felt like I needed a nap.

This was also the first time I had seen her naked. I was attracted to her. She was beautiful, stubborn and lilting at the same time; she was a walking, talking lemon drop. But when I saw her naked that first time, walking across the room in the afternoon light, I was disappointed. It all seemed so different when I was tasting her saliva, and feeling her body against mine with eyes closed. Everything was so new, and I had been swept away with my own flush of romance. I wasn't quite ready to reconcile the figurative feel of her with the literal, functional impression of her body, looking for a condom in her dresser like it was a kitchen cupboard.

When she came back to bed with a handful of condoms, I started to panic. I realized I had lost my half-erection during the minute she had been gone. I took the condoms out of her hand and pulled her back into bed, hoping that kissing and foreplay would get my lazy afternoon boner back. This was my first encounter with the vortex of the disappearing boner. As soon as you're conscious of the fact that it's gone, the fixation on its continuing absence hangs over your head like a cackling crow. Every minute or so my subconscious would bubble up, 'Nope, still no erection.'

After much straining, angst, and a blowjob, I finally forced my mule back into his yolk. I tenuously slipped the condom down over my penis, torturing myself with the idea that this one would melt away like the one before it. There's a lot of pressure involved in having a penis. If men put hideously unreasonable expectations on women by validating sexual tripe like Playboy and Hooters, the converse is that we've boxed ourselves into a role of being rock-steady pipe layers. Virility served 24 hours a day or my name isn't Joe Namath.

The most distressing part of my penile performance over the last few years has been a gradually increasing refractory period. But I've noticed that I want to switch positions more frequently now. A little too long spent in one posture and I start to lose track. A brief image of my penis made out of quicksand flashes through my head, and that's enough to sharpen my fear.

Then I wonder, what will things be like in five years? Or 10 years? Will I start popping hard-on pills when I'm forty and my mule is more interested in grazing? Would it be insulting to my partner if my erections became more scattershot? Can you have sex without penetration? Can intimacy and eroticism take a form outside of the throbbing masthead without being somehow less? I'm a little bit frightened of the idea of having a teenage erection attached to my wrinkly, liver-spotted 50-year-old body. When I was young I had sex like a young man. As I get older, it doesn't seem unnatural that sex should change accordingly.

I just don't know what that means. How do old men have sex?

Does My Butt Show When I Walk?

I had a pressing need to venture into the heart of the East Bay suburbs one weekend to find a Target. I rode BART to the end of the line in Richmond. I was about to move to New York and had decided I should bring N some handmade ice cream from Bi-Rite Creamery, packed in a camping cooler and dry ice to survive the cross-country flight. But I needed a cooler first. I had never been to Richmond but my friend told me that all my retail needs would be taken care of in that mythic borderland where the city meets the suburban sprawl.

I got off the train in a gray drizzle and soon realized I was in the middle of nowhere. There was a sign announcing this was Downtown Richmond, but all I could see was a Burger King, some empty office buildings, and long corridors of stucco apartment buildings reaching towards the horizon.

I started walking toward the Burger King, hoping it would be the start of a commercial trail of cookie crumbs that would lead me to Target. I was wrong. I kept getting further and further into a residential kaleidoscope. There wasn't anyone out on the sidewalks, the streets were lined with ramshackle houses hemmed in with cold chain link fences.

I zig-zagged through the neighborhood for an hour, feeling my tether to the BART station stretch as I went. Richmond reminded me of Fresno, the Central Valley town where I grew up. It was peaceful, unassuming, and deathly quiet. You could see someone walking towards you from a quarter mile away and minutes would pass as you watched each other draw closer, tense and uncertain.

I went back to Fresno a couple years ago, taking pictures for a movie project that fell apart. I stopped at the neighborhood grocery store in the afternoon to get some water. It felt smaller than when I was a teenager, like a toy approximation of what I had been expecting. I walked past the bakery and someone called my name.

I looked behind the counter and saw a cross-eyed women with frizzy hair barely contained under a hairnet. She had crooked teeth and a black eye. 'You don't remember me, do you?' she said as I walked towards her.

'I don't think so,' I told her, trying to place her face. It was pale and riddled with liver spots under the harsh lighting.

'I was your second grade teacher!' she said. 'I remember you.'

I had a faint memory of my second grade teacher, but it was impossible to match this woman with that silhouetted shape. I was tiny then, and the orbit of my life was barely a blip, happily filled with the sugar rushes of childhood delight. The world was above me and I felt like I was gradually rising to meet it, a watery mirage waiting on the other side of the surface.

Then here was my teacher, cross-eyed somehow, bruised and withering (I kept wondering who in her life could have given her a black eye), baking cakes with industrial-sized equipment in a chain supermarket. The more we talked the less I could reconcile our past and present states. I felt like I was watching someone drown while being drawn further and further away.

As I was walking back to the BART station, defeated in my attempt to find Target, I walked into a narrow pedestrian alley through an underpass. I saw a woman ahead of me, stubby and round, sauntering through the walkway in heels and a tight mini-skirt. As she walked the mini-skirt rode up her hips until her buttocks were drooping onto her dappled upper thighs.

She was walking slowly and I was catching up to her. The smell of piss and car exhaust was trapped in the underpass. When I was a few feet away she turned around as if she knew I had been there the whole time.

'Can I ask you a question? Does my butt show when I walk?' she asked. It looked like she was grinning to herself.

It did, but I didn't want to tell her so I lied. 'No, not that I can see.'

I asked her if she knew where the Target was. She said I was still a long way away, 20 blocks down. I knew she was lying. She smiled at me, it felt lascivious and confrontational.

On the other side of the underpass I peeled away toward the BART station and she kept walking straight ahead, wobbling on her heels and in no rush to get anywhere. Her butt was still showing. And I was still looking at it.

Let Me Seduce You with The Cardigans

I was in college the first time I heard 'Love Fool' at my friend R's apartment. She was drunk and really stoned when she put it on. The first thing she did when it started playing was apologize for having chosen it. I liked the song fine, but I also wasn't really paying attention. The rise to fame on the sparkling froth of that song made it easy to dismiss The Cardigans as some producer's invention. A few years later I ducked into a coffee shop to get out of a rainstorm while living in Prague and heard First Band on the Moon playing on the stereo. I listened to it while sipping black coffee, trapped indoors, waiting on the weather to lighten up. That's when I realized that I like The Cardigans.

I liked the self-deprecating lilt in Nina Persson's voice and the straight-laced fuzz pop that played beneath it. When I heard their version of 'Iron Man', like a dilated pastel lullaby of original's rusted metal angst, I was convinced. It was surprising to listen to a band that I had already dismissed and find something that I responded to. 'Does this mean I like bad music?' I wondered to myself.

I remember when confessed my affection for The Cardigans to N, trying to explain the allure of Persson's confrontationally vulnerable lyrics. I euphemistically invited her back to my apartment to 'listen' to The Cardigans. She rolled her eyes. At my place I had to turn off the Cardigans record after two songs because it was too distracting.

I've got a long history of getting attached to crappy music. I wore out my Milli Vanilli tape in high school. Long after the controversy about the fake singing had subsided I kept listening to the cornflake pop, indulging my teenage yearnings with their glossy sledgehammer of musical emotion. My affection for The Cardigans is probably closer to that indulgence than I care to admit. It's easy to look back a few years and dismiss who you once were based on inexperience and stupidity, but it's something else to do that in the present tense. When I was single and stuck in Prague through the dreary gray months of a winter, that music had been like a sparkling diamond.

Years later, in a new room, hearing all of that defeated indulgence was embarrassing. It wasn't that the music was so bad, but more that I had underestimated how I had changed in the intervening years. It was like trying to have sex with someone surrounded by a wallpaper of embarrassing pictures of my high school self. We were on the way to having sex, but suddenly felt like I was trapped in a wallowing flashback from an unhappier time.

Listening to music with other people is such a different experience than listening to it alone. When you're with someone else music is meant to stay out of the way, to be a subconscious lubricant. Alone it becomes physical. It gains intensity and layers of meaning that aren't there when your attention is trained on someone else. Playing The Cardigans was like trying to give someone a gift that I really just wanted for myself. It was selfish and stupid.

So instead, I put on 'Fantasy' by Mariah Carey. N climbed on top of me and rapped along to the ODB breakdown and I was as smitten as I've ever been with anyone. I had never listened to the lyrics before that night. I still remember the first line, hearing it in duplicate tumbling from her lips like a begrudging confession of her own stake in the song, her embarrassed smile levitating below her eyes, drifting away toward the ceiling, singing by instinct. Me and Mariah go back like babies and pacifiers. Swoon.

Tom Brady's Love Handles

As the 2008 NFL season began, news broke that Tom Brady, the man-hunk quarterback for the New England Patriots, used to have love handles. Some guy that owns a pizza place in some random Palookaville that Brady once danced through on his way to Olympus was been quoted as saying the college-age Brady used to eat ham and cheese grinders with a fatty side of onion rings. To back the claim, a shirtless photo has surfaced of Brady from his rookie weigh-in with the slender but doughy physique of a cubicle surfer.

I imagine stories like this satisfy some need for prurient gloating. This specimen of raw male ambrosia used to be the regular guy in old gym shorts nursing cheesy fries at the end of your dorm hallway. The key to Tom Brady the sex symbol is his body; the key to Tom Brady the regular guy is the layer of fat gently covering over his physiology with the faintest hint of sloth and youthful gluttony.

That schism is disturbing to me. The sex god Tom Brady, with his hulking triceps, hairy chest, and chiseled jaw might as well be an animatronic sex doll. That's not a slur on the human being the doll was based on; I have no idea who he is (though he has at least partially consented to this presentation of himself as a glossy object of desire, based exclusively on physiology). Attractive people are nice to look at and all, but there's something pathetic about the creation of some superhuman version of a person just to stoke the interest of the culturati who need a new pet name for their vibrators.

I realize protesting about the image of Tom Brady is sort of absurd because this kind of dehumanization through sexual iconography has been the yoke born by women in the public spotlight for years, decades, centuries, and millennia. There's nothing particularly tragic about Tom Brady's ascension to swank material. But it did remind me of feet.

I hate feet in general. I can't think of anyone I know off-hand that I would say has nice feet. I have one lovely friend who has an unfortunately permanent toenail fungus who takes great pleasure in torturing me with her feet. Feet are the part on a person's body where things inevitably fall apart and begin to decay. It surprised me how much I miss N's feet in the months after she left. She didn't have particularly nice feet, but I sometimes found myself staring off into odd corners remembering the knobby pink bunions on her third toes. I missed them. I still miss them.

It's not the body that matters. It's what the body says about the person, how it comes to be an effigy to the spirit inside after you've come to know someone. In the glut of celebrity media that has come to embody our aesthetics and consumerism, we've somehow lost track of the fact that there are actually people inside of those blank celebrity automatons moving across the pages of People magazine. We punish celebrities for breaking from their idealized image. But the image is always the least interesting part of anything; a person, a place, or a moment in time. So take the time, for a moment, to enjoy the gap between rookie-Tom and the man who's become Giselle Bundchen's real life vibrator. I hardly know you, Tom, and I hardly even care.

Chest Hair, or the Shaved Eunuch

My dad grew a beard when he was in his mid-20s. I used to look at old pictures of him when I was growing up and imagine one day filling out a body that was similar to his. I expected a bushy mustache as if it were a birthright.

I waited patiently through college and into my early 20s, expecting an explosion of hair. I watched my older brother experiment with a pubic goatee and wondered if my facial hair would look similarly disgusting when it finally appeared. The hairs around my nipples grew longer and multiplied. I began to notice a long nose hair emerging from my left nostril. But the thick and burly hair I was waiting for never arrived.

Today I shave twice a week. My chest is a pale, barren plane. I want to imbue some kind of meaning into that, but since I stopped expecting my body to somehow change into something it won't ever be I don't see what meaning it could have. Body hair is another safe thing to fixate on when trying to articulate what you want. It's easiest to identify body parts that might be attached to any random person. Chest hair doesn't have a face.

And still I wonder sometimes what my body might be like with more hair. The specter of a six o'clock shadow hangs over my entire wardrobe and some nights I'm a twinge disappointed to look in the mirror and see my flushed pink skin where coarse, manly texture should be. I used to wonder what my chest would be like with hair, wishing that I could have given a lover the muskier version of my body, with a sultry matting of bed-warmed chest hair to nuzzle in.

Those are the kinds of thought experiments I would dismiss outright from a woman. I don't like hypotheticals about the bodies of people I'm sleeping with. I don't want to think of someone I care about in terms of physical aggregation. You don't fuck body parts.

With my own body, I have a double standard. It's my ego, and I want it to be in everything, a vessel for every possible experience another person could want. I want to believe in a world where I could the giving center of everything for someone, but instead all I have is my hairless body. Elbows and shoulder blades, with some long nipple hair for irony's sake.

Who is Lauren Cohan and Why Is She Hitting On Me?

I've never slept with a celebrity. Not that it matters. The people we tend to celebrate as stars are almost always entertainers. I definitely appreciate the art of performance, but I don't understand the continuing necessity of elevating actors to some quasi-celestial status. They contribute to society in the form of entertainment, by uniting us at our lowest common denominator. They don't create, they make believe. As Ian McKellan put it once, 'How did I know what to say? The words were written down for me in a script. How did I know where to stand? People told me.'

So then, one night, when I still lived in Hollywood, I was out for a drink with a friend at Coach and Horses (now closed, closed, closed). The bar was mostly empty. P and I drank Pabst tall boys and listened to The Misfits on the jukebox, arguing about some arcane cinema minutiae. After an hour, two women came in and set themselves at the far end of the bar. There was a blonde who, despite all her physical symmetry, still looked like morning breath to me. The second woman was a skinny brunette in a loose silk shirt with had a hint of rodentia about her face.

Both women were pretty, but I generally don't care about pretty. I try not to think too hard about the people I'm attracted to. Either there's something beyond my power of understanding that compels me to speak, or there isn't. I appreciate prettiness but, like acting, I don't really see the long-lasting value in it. If there's no ripple in the air underneath the well arranged face then who cares.

So I went back to deconstructing Maborosi or whatever stupendously important film I was in the midst of prancing over, when the rodent lady walked over to us. 'Excuse me, I've been dying to have a kind gentleman buy me a glass of champagne all night,' she said. Great, the pretty woman in the empty bar is going to spend the rest of the night harvesting drinks from us. Pretty or not, I generally am disinclined to paying for conversation with strangers, even as a demonstration of good faith. If someone wants to talk with you, extracting $10 from your wallet should never serve as precursor.

P, however, is not half the chilly bastard that I can be with strange women and he waved the bartender over so that champagnes could be discussed. After some verbal pitter-patter it came out that this woman was an actor and had been in Van Wilder 2: The Rise of Taj. It's rare enough that a woman hits on me in public (for a free drink or otherwise), but entirely unheard of when the woman hitting on me is a celebrity.

It's debatable whether or not the lead from Van Wilder 2 qualifies as a celebrity or not. Photos of her walking out of a Starbucks with a terrier in her purse aren't burning up TMZ, but in terms of contribution to the world, she's got to be in the same category as any of the more tint-eyed women clotting up our magazines. To me she's a celebrity.

P played right into her, flirting and asking her leading questions. I listened to them talk and tossed out dismissive one-liners here and there. 'You know, your friends kind of an asshole,' she said about me after I made a joke about actors (if Hitchcock can call them cattle, I don't seen why they can't be fodder for jokes in good company). And telling someone you were the lead actor in Van Wilder 2 is a pretty good beginning to a hustle. How many people have actually seen Van Wilder 2?

But so anyway, I realized that P was giving Lauren his hard sell and I was probably hurting his chances so I decided to shut up. I started talking to the bartender and let P and Lauren work things out. That took about three minutes and then Lauren took her free champagne and went back to her friend.

Still skeptical about the whole thing, I looked up Van Wilder 2 as soon as I got home. There was Lauren's face, staring right back at me from the monitor. She really was an actor. A few images down the Google search I saw some naked stills someone had harvested from the movie. Reader, I have no excuse for what happened next, but I confess I masturbated to pictures of Lauren Cohan naked after having derided her in real life an hour earlier. It's strange that I wouldn't spring for a drink for her, but I would still fantasize about stripping down with her.

This is primarily why I don't trust beauty or celebrity. There seems to be a Pavlovian connection between the idea of it and the need to compulsively gratify one's sexuality (at least my home-alone-on-a-Sunday-night-sexuality). Celebrities are wonderful Kewpie dolls to preoccupy our spare mental energy with, but for all the energy we reflexively spend thinking about their love lives, political causes, and career choices, they're just actors in a bar trying to hustle a free drink on a slow night. While I remained the self-flagellating bastard making fun of them.

Willing to Relocate

I'd never thought about moving for someone before N. During my most desperate throes of love the idea of giving up vocation and place for a girlfriend was an abstraction at best. I fantasized about diving in front of stray gunfire in slow motion to protect them; I pictured myself warding off packs of armed muggers in dark alleyways absorbing macho bruises to keep them from danger. But I never contemplated risking anything real.

I finally moved a year after I'd met N. A mutual friend had an Easter brunch at his apartment. He and N were matched against each other in a pancake-off. He was making chocolate buckwheat pancakes and hers were banana walnut.

I had been in San Francisco a little over three months. My new job was transitioning from a surreal delight into a time-consuming challenge. By Sunday morning I was feeling tired and selfish. I remember thinking I looked like shit. I had just conditioned my hair and it was puffy and frizzy.

I was wearing a pair of beige corduroy pants and a white-knit polo shirt with thin horizontal stripes that was too small for me. It was short and too tight in the arms but the midsection shot out in an angular waddle that I didn't like. The pants were a little too short and I was wearing black ankle socks that were uncomfortably apparent when I sat down.

When I arrived, my friend led me through his shotgun apartment to the kitchen where everybody else was waiting. That was where I saw N for the first time. Her back was to me. She was wearing a pink thrift store sundress and a white apron. I saw the pale skin of her calves, blotchy in the cold March air. I saw her black and wavy hair coming down over her shoulders.

When she moved to New York, I fell apart. I remember the day she left. I invented some reason to take the morning off from work so I could stay with her right up until the moment she had to leave. We spent the night at my apartment, woke up to a bright and sunny day and walked back to her old place. I remember walking that path many times over those two months. I was always getting off work late, but I would walk those dirty sidewalks as fast as I could to meet her almost every night of the week.

We were quiet that morning. I smoked one of her cigarettes on the way. We held hands. I teased her, wanting to pretend that this was another normal day. Half an hour later we got to her apartment. It was getting close to noon. We stopped at the threshold to her front door. I didn't know what to say. I had known that she was leaving from the beginning. We weren't going to be able to stay together.

I knew that moment was coming, but I had ignored it. We faced each other and held both hands. I kissed her and held on for a few seconds. 'It's going to be hard to let you go,' I told her.

She was quiet. If she said anything, I don't remember it.

We kissed one last time and I started walking back down the sidewalk. I turned around and watched her. She looked at me and then started putting the key in the lock of the front gate. I turned around again at the corner of the block, but she had gone inside already. The threshold in front of her building was empty.

When I started writing for Nerve she asked me never to write about her. 'If I wind up on there, you're a dead man,' she told me.

She's been in every story I've written. Sometimes it's been literal, other times she's been in the blank spaces between words, the invisible center around which all these little black letters orbit.

I know it's stupid to think about someone in those terms. People aren't centers of gravity. She's just a woman. At the end of all these strung out words, like loose strands of thread, there's just a woman waiting. She has cuticles and calluses and plaque and eye boogers and dirty fingernails. She watches CSI and owns a Jack Johnson record, She's just another person, in a world of other people.

And there I was, with my bags packed and a one-way ticket to New York City. I had no idea what would happen when I got there. It's tempting to think of relationships as an answer to something. I wanted to imagine that I was reaching a finish line, that I was finally ready to confront the metaphysical truth with my metaphysical doppleganger. That's what everyone wants, isn't it? The one. To find that person you're willing to put it all on the line for, the albino unicorn galloping into the sea.

Life doesn't get easier and simpler. It expands, becomes more complicated. I was scared to the point of numbness. I had a lot of good rhetorical reasons for moving. I'd wanted to move to New York since I was a teenager. I had a lot of lovely friends in the city and while I knew I would be broke and couch surfing there would be a bounty of new opportunities to chase after.

But that wasn't why I'm moved. I moved because I was in love. (I'm still in love) I'm moving for N. Whatever happens between us, I didn't want to have felt what I feel for her and not stood up for it.

I don't know what the weight of my life is worth. I don't know why I exist or what benefit can come out of it. But I do know who I love. I knew before I saw her face, I knew it then, and I know it now. She has dark wavy hair, calluses, dirty fingernails, a Jack Johnson record, and some questionable taste in television programming.

I wrote about getting text messages from her being inevitable while she was in San Francisco, like watching a wave building out on the ocean before slowly coming to shore. I had nothing to lose then. I was the stationary one, sitting passively on the shore, feeling the wet rush from each swell crashing against the sand.

When I moved it felt like I was becoming the wave out at sea. I feel myself rushing and swelling toward her, a stationary figure waiting on the shore, watching me come apart in a foamy haze as gravity pulled me closer.

For a few wet seconds it was like I was levitating.

How Soon, Sex Toy?

I got a cock ring for my birthday a few years ago. I had never considered using a sex toy for my own benefit before. Sex toys are an implicit taboo for straight men. It's become generally accepted that women benefit from vibrators and dildos for their own self-pleasure (how could a woman get off without a phallus?), but a man with a sex toy is a greasy kink monster.

One of the benefits of being in a relationship is that you are given leeway to experiment with new ways to arouse yourself and your partner. Sex toys lose their fetishistic edge and become more functional and exploratory. They aren't lurid artifacts but new intermediaries with which to break new ground. Being single is a different matter. How can you reasonably try and break new ground with someone when you're only vaguely acquainted with their body and person?

I used to tease N that we could use a truck battery and alligator clips together. 'It'll be our thing, just for me and you,' I told her. 'We're not using alligator clips,' she would tell me with a deadpan glare.

I've never used an electrical current during sex, and my offer wasn't serious. But the irony wasn't meant to be totally dismissive either. I know what's felt good to me in the past, but I can't say what will elicit that reaction tomorrow. In the worst of times, we get so familiar with ourselves, and the bodies in bed with us, that we forget to move forward. We tell each other myths about 'good' sex and 'bad' sex, and then assemble a mountain of books, websites, seminars, and television shows to create a rubric for it.

Sex is both mundane and ecstatic. It is fundamentally unknowable. The more familiar it becomes the more it loses its defining quality. Which is a lot to saddle a lover with, servicing the mundanity and ecstasy of our bodies. Can a person's imagination really be so expansive as to keep the act a continual discovery, day after day or year after year?

I also own anal beads, though I have never used them with anyone else. I'm not sure I like using them on myself. I like the attempt, it's an experience I've never had before. I fumble and do things awkwardly; it's not the most intuitive of processes and is even less so without an extra set of hands. But it's an adventure, something I'm happy to have embarked on.

At what point does the introduction of sex accoutrements become acceptable with a new partner? Is there a dictum requiring polite society to avoid anal beads until the third date? Is the use of a cock ring a masochistic affront to a man's hetero-virility?

I bought another woman I had dated a vibrating dildo once. It sounds like an easy task, but I wandered around the back of the sex store for an hour debating different shapes, sizes, and functions. Would it have been rude to buy a big ten-inch dildo? Would it have been sad to present her with the narrow five inch one instead? Whatever my choice, it would be up to her to make the best use of it. We had stopped seeing each other earlier and so my seat on the exploratory committee had been abdicated.

I settled on something pink and soft, with a gentle motor and a modest length. I played it safe, not wanting to push the line with something crass and swollen. Later, she told me she had used it for a few months and thrown it away. I should have gotten her something that connected to a truck battery. Or better yet, we should have gone shopping together, before we stopped having sex.

Crying In Public: My Cubicle

I don't cry all that easily. I remember being on a date with a girl in high school (we went to see My Life with Michael Keaton and Nichole Kidman) and trying hard to make myself cry toward the end. I thought somehow it would complete the image of a sensitive guy that I was trying so hard to project. It didn't work. I cried for an hour straight when that same girl left town a year later. But that happened in the privacy of my own bedroom.

Over the years I've found myself crying in public more than in private. One such place was my cubicle at work the day N moved. I had to stay late playing Grand Theft Auto IV. I needed to finish the game in a short amount of time and explain to the anonymous masses why it was a thin and hollow creation, waddling in sarcasm and cynicism. It was 8PM and I was alone, hungry, and just beginning to fully absorb what it would really mean for N to be gone, while trying to pay attention to a cutscene about Russians and Irishmen feuding over heroin or diamonds. Things were not going well.

Then I got to a segment where I drove around in a car whose radio stations I could change. One of the stations was playing 'Flashing Lights' by Kanye West. GTA is set in gritty, hyper-real version of New York. Driving through the polygon neighbor-hoods, draped in green-gray textures, broken by hopeless brown-stones and grimy subway overpasses listening to that song I realized that she had gone somewhere I couldn't follow. So I started crying.

The first time I ever heard 'Flashing Lights' was with her and I remember not liking it very much. After a few more listens I recall going on an over-long diatribe about how lacking the rhymes were, pontificating about how stupid it was for West to connect Mona Lisa and Cesar. How clever! Then I started to hear the song everywhere, the way popular songs suddenly seem to populate every background like an overwhelming swarm. I didn't like it until, one day, I decided I liked the song a lot, if only because it reminded me of N and the pleasure of orating in front of her patiently deadpan face. She was patient during these moments. She seemed to understand that I didn't actually care about the point I was making but simply needed to react, to convulse verbally at some provocation, to feel words forming in my brain and then see how many of them I could throw out in an improvised moment before talking myself in a dead end. She seemed to be watching me more than she was listening to me in those moments, and I loved her for it.

It wasn't long before I had the whole album in heavy rotation on my iPod. I began looking up lyrics from it and wondered if there were ways to work Kanye West quotes into my articles. It was a standard musical dalliance and she left right in the middle of it. Songs can become little bits of broken glass, that have some elliptical image or angle of the past in them. It's not the music, but the way it catches a glimpse of some place you used to be, some person you used to know, one particular letter in the alphabet. The letter N. When I heard the opening violin trills of 'Flashing Lights' come out of my TV speakers while driving through the gray-brown landscape of fake Brooklyn I realized how horribly sad I was about her being gone. Horribly, awfully, irrevocably. And I started crying at work.

Moving to New York and Where It Got Me

It was lucky that we met. When I look back, it seems impossible that I ever would have met N. Of all the things that had to fall into place, all the plans I made that didn't work out, all the unexpected offers that led me into places I never though I'd wanted to go; at every step, one little change would have meant none of this would have happened.

If I'd been accepted at conservatory when I was 18; if I'd skipped the poetry workshop my sophomore year of college where my friend H planted the idea of interning at a movie production company; if I'd been accepted in the trainee program at the management company instead of leaving for Peace Corps; if I'd been hired at one of the random office jobs in LA I'd tried so desperately to get when I came back; if I'd taken my prejudice against San Francisco seriously and never moved there; if I'd decided to stay home that Easter because I was tired and didn't feel like socializing; there are so many little details that could have thrown it all off. It was luck.

Before I met N, I thought I knew myself well enough. I had been through a lot, had fended for myself, taken lots of risks without any clear payoffs waiting ahead. I knew what I wanted out of life and I had a clear understanding of what I was going to have to go through to get it. I knew what I had to share with a partner and I knew what I would expect in return.

One of the first things I learned about N when we met was that she was moving to New York in two months. When we went out on our first real date I knew there was another man waiting for her in New York.

A week later we made plans to go out again. I was scared. I called my friend C and told her what was happening. We were about to start something overwhelming and inarticulate. It was like watching a whale coming up from under the ocean. I saw the smooth, alien surface rising just above the water and had no idea what it was. But I knew that it was big. I had already decided to go with it, but I was afraid of that choice. I wanted C to make sense of it for me; to tell me why I was going to do what I was about to do.

As N's departure drew closer I didn't feel like I could do anything other than loosen my fingers and watch her slide away. That end had been beside us during every second we were together, even when I consciously turned my back on it. And when she left I watched her go.

N is the love of my life. When I was finally able to say that out loud without feeling embarrassed about it, I decided to move to New York. I wanted to give her everything. That's why I moved. This is all I have to give someone. And I brought it to her.

We hadn't gotten back together. We talked. We went out together sometimes. When we were together it still felt like it did. But that wasn't enough.

I'd been lying to myself about the move since I decided months before I tried to describe it in pure rhetorical terms. 'This is all I have to give someone.' That sentiment describes the amorphous emotion that's propelled me all this way, but it's an incomplete description. It's a sentence fragment.

I didn't just come to give her something. I came to take something, I came to ask her to give me something back. Like giving someone a birthday present and watching expectantly as they unwrap it, there was an unspoken expectation in my coming here. I didn't want to acknowledge that part. I didn't want to say that part out loud. I don't want to be that needy one, that demanding one. But I am.

When I wrote about coming here last month I said N had black hair. It's not true. She has brown hair. I was wrong. I moved across the country for a woman whose hair color I couldn't even get right.

One night after I got here we had a fight. We were supposed

to meet for drinks but she was in the middle of a busy week and had been out late the night before. I felt wounded. 'I can handled not being your boyfriend, not being your sweetheart,' I texted her. 'But I can't handle feeling like an albatross, an asterisk appending your real life.'

How is somebody supposed to make another person not feel like an asterisk? How can anyone ask another person to make them feel differently about themselves? For all my opaque rhetoric about wanting only to give to her, here I was wearing my wounded emotions on my sleeve and wondering why she won't do more to fix them.

I'd given up on every woman I'd ever been in love with. I never fought for any of them, I never tried to make a case, never made a show of what I could give them besides a passive and easy-going friendship. When you fall in love with someone you ask them to sacrifice for you. You ask them to amend their plans for the future to include you, to forgo all the new experiences they might have had with other romances, to never experience another person's body after your own. It's cruel. It's a prison.

'I wish we understood each other better,' she told me a few days after I got here. 'I am often surprised about it both ways, how we do and don't.'

I don't know how this is supposed to end. There isn't an answer buried in any of this. There is no ending.

I remember looking at her in a bar my second week in the city. We were talking about music. I had just finished tearing down The Soft Bulletin by The Flaming Lips. It was grating and overly saccharine. She told me it was about Wayne's father dying of cancer, the adolescent dregs of superhero fantasy turned into a coping mechanism for the inevitable parting of everyone you'll ever love. We went to see The Reader. I laughed the whole way through. I was filled with incredulity for the stodgy camera angles, the baroque dialogue, and the hackneyed soap opera plot. She liked the actor who played the young boy. She saw past the surface, the stupid superficial flaws, and found the pretty parts underneath. She left the theater with those. I left with my own stupid punchlines and in-jokes.

I admire her as much as anyone I've ever known. She's strong in all the places where I would come apart. She listens where I'd jump in to filibuster and orate. She's direct and unapologetic where I'd talk in circles and avoid having to answer.

It was lucky we met. I wish I had more to give to her than this, my wounded feelings and dusty luggage.

I remember one of the first nights we went out together in San Francisco. I invited her to come to a friend's birthday party with me. We had seen each other twice before. I had been in her bed and we had kissed for almost two hours on her front step. Still, I was nervous when I went over to her apartment to pick her up. I didn't know where we stood with each other yet. I was afraid I liked her too much.

We walked down the sidewalk toward my friend's place. We stopped at the big intersection by Church and Market waiting for the signal. We were both looking straight ahead at the red circle shining in its black metal housing across the street.

I tried to look at her without turning my head. I could feel her body next to me in the cold night air. It was like a little ball of soft energy. It was good.

The light was getting ready to change. I could feel the seconds moving by. We would have to start walking forward again soon. I leaned down towards without looking, then turned my head and kissed her on the cheek.

I stood back upright and looked straight ahead again, watching the stoplight. After a couple of seconds I looked at her again. She kept staring straight ahead, but a smile spread across her lips as she felt me looking at her. The light turned green. 'Come on,' she said. I put my arm around her shoulders and we stepped into the crosswalk.

The Seductive Art of Dancing

During my first week in New York I went to see a band called Starfucker play in Brooklyn. Everything they played was danceable, and the small basement room was filled with sweaty people bopping to the click and pulse of the music.

There was a man near the front of the stage who danced throughout the whole set. He was wearing an old t-shirt and a Holden Caulfield hunting cap. He was a little chubby and pale but he moved with a selflessness that was endearing, almost encouraging. I felt self-conscious about not dancing when I looked at him.

A few years earlier I had met an ex-bagboy with anger management issues who had just finished a year stay at a Buddhist monastery. He was thin and soft-spoken. He looked perpetually sunburned and had a blushing smile that he seemed to wrestle with in fits of embarrassment.

He once told me that women can tell if you're good at sex by how well you dance. He opened his eyes a little wider and tried to suppress that blushing smile when he confessed that a woman he knew had told him he was a good dancer.

I like to dance. I used to feel self-conscious about it. I would only do it in private or, if I was drunk enough, with a woman in a crowded party. When I was 23 my friend P told me to shut up and just two-step to everything. A girl I used to date suggested that I dance like a praying mantis, all gangly angles and insectoid gestures.

I'm not sure if that's true or not. I am long and thin. There's a fine line between grace and loping angularity with a frame like mine. Some nights are less graceful than others.

I've stopped believing that there's a good or bad way to dance. Dancing is like sex in that it's an expression and shouldn't ever become an act of assimilating to a set of best common practices.

It's easy to imagine there's a right way to dance because it preys on the nascent social anxieties we all have.

With sex, everyone's certain they're an above-average lover. Everyone seems to have osmotically absorbed those best common practices, but with dancing, and especially for men, the best common practice is to confess incompetence. 'No, I can't. I'm a terrible dancer,' we tell each other. Imagine if you were sleeping with someone the first time and they declined to go down on you, claiming that they're really terrible at oral.

So but there I was in a basement in Brooklyn, watching another man dance because he liked the band so much that his body had to move with them. He looked perfectly in place in short bursts, like the impossibly joyful crowds on a New Year's Eve special dancing along to a Pink song in their Macy's best. The longer I watched him the clumsier he became. He was off-beat and barely moving his hands. He turned in slow circles, making eye contact with everyone around him but his body was little more than off-kilter pendulum in a furry hunting hat.

I wanted to join him. I wanted to dance alongside him, to feel that same immediate need to let my body speak because it was filled with happiness.

But I couldn't. I just wasn't that into the band.

Taking A Break From Dating

I started talking to a woman at a party in San Francisco a few months before I moved to New York. She confessed that she was taking a break from dating. I was immediately excited. I wanted her to hurry up and finish her explanation of how she had come to a point of general exhaustion in her dating life so that I could add my own thoughts. I'm taking a break too! It was a thrill to have found such immediate common ground with someone I had only met a few minutes before. Everyone I knew at the party had gone home early. I had turned to the closest person I could find to strike up a conversation hoping to stave off going home early on a Saturday night. I didn't want to seem like I was hitting on her, so when the opportunity arose to disavow any immediate participation in the mating rituals of urban city dweller I felt giddy.

The idea that one can take a break from dating seems self-indulgent. It's like saying you're going to take a break from ice cream. Dating isn't easy, and it can feel like work, but it's always interesting. Even when it's boring, you can always learn something new about people or how you relate to them. And the possibility of romance sparking underneath the surface, like some exposed electrical wire, is exciting.

But it's a privilege to be able to apply so much time and energy to finding a partner who'll fulfill some romantic ideal. I always wonder about the comparative success of arranged marriages compared to the staggering divorce rates in the unarranged world. I wonder if it isn't entirely reckless to believe that you can select your own mate using a divining rod whose most important criterion is love. Looking at marriage as an effective partnership between two people who agree to set aside personal agendas for the sake of a family is painfully anti-climactic. But it's statistically more likely to hold fast than the woozy promises made under a lovespell on a hot summer night.

One of the most rewarding things about being in Peace Corps was seeing how quickly and totally all the socially constructed barriers between people can be broken down. I remember the first day showing up for staging and looking around the hotel conference room at the rabble of oat-fed college graduates looking at the bullet points on a government-issue whiteboard. I couldn't believe I had traded my real friends and family for this group of sandal-wearing do-gooders. It was repulsive to imagine I was leaving behind a life I had so carefully built for this random group of people who were so earnest and idealistic that they almost should have been wearing helmets.

A few weeks later we might as well have all been menstruating on the same lunar cycle. Stripped of country, companionship, language, and possessions, the need for trust and intimacy become irrepressible; like the unavoidable urgency of oxygen when you've been underwater for too long. Bonds form and love grows like a flower sprouted in cow shit, no less strong or real for its crass beginnings.

Sometimes dating feels like hurling yourself against another person's outer barriers over and over again. Both sides want the closeness, acceptance, and intimacy, and neither side trusts the other will be able to provide them. So we fixate on politics and fashion, deconstruct taste in music or movies, and use them as barriers to keep from having to offer someone empathy. We circle each other in bars and coffee shops, evaluating, approaching, and dismissing; as if love were something you simply find and not something you give.

I was just about to start telling all of this to the woman at the party, the pudgy one with horn-rimmed glasses who I was worried would think I was hitting on her. Twenty seconds after I told her I was taking a break from dating, she excused herself to go outside for a cigarette. I looked around the room and didn't see anyone I recognized. So I left.

Loyal as a Dog

According to convention, men are dogs and no more loyal than their current options. I don't like the stereotype. It makes me tighten my lips and flatten my toes against the insides of my shoes. So there must be some truth to it. I've noticed that I sometimes have a wandering eye when I'm with women. Walking down the sidewalk arm in arm or sharing a table in a coffee shop somewhere, the jingle of the door opening and the stirring of color in the periphery draws my attention away. When that periphery blur becomes a visible woman I am drawn even further into a look, like some dog hearing a distant barking.

Men are always looking to trade up, comedy teaches us. They are satisfied with their partners so long as they don't have to face the fact that they might have gotten a better deal somewhere else. But what actually constitutes a better deal? What is it that a man is wondering he'll find when his left eye catches on a passing woman?

If men are dogs then they can't be looking to trade up. Dogs are creatures of territory and powerful associations with a pack. I had two dogs growing up and I doubt either of them would have gone AWOL from our family home had they been tempted with a new home in the mountains with an endless supply of fresh bones to gnaw on and open lawn stretching to the horizon. One word from my father, one whistle, one jingle of the leash and they would have come sprinting back home with happy tongues flapping out of their mouths.

It's impossible to erase the instinctual tether of home from a dog's mind but they are easily distracted. I, too, am often wracked by distractions. The number of times I have opened and closed Facebook while writing these modest few paragraphs borders on dysfunctional. The same impulsive urge to toss a glance elsewhere is no less powerful in public. I immediately feel guilty for it. Sometimes I'll force myself to not look, to keep my line of sight trained directly on the woman I'm with, becoming distracted with my own rigidity in the process.

Is it an insult to look at other women, or men, when you're with someone? Is it an insinuation of disloyalty, the psychic tic of a wandering libido?

I can't think of staying with someone in terms of options. I understand the logic behind the idea, but it is incongruous with every impulse I've ever had when with a woman. Everyone is surrounded with options, on all sides. Everyone walks out their door in the morning and passes someone else on the street that they could sleep with or date. Having options is hard work. Options can lead to opportunities, but those opportunities require effort, articulation of a specific desire, and some final kind of making. Every option is a risk in its own way.

Some women are upset by knowing their men look around. They want to feel like their company is enough to consume their man's attention. His curious energies should all be applied toward her, or else something safe and innocuous, like the boat in the backyard or college sports.

I don't know why I look at other women. But I always look back again. The glance is never more than a second or two, before disinterest settles in. I look away, sending my eyes out over the vast lawn, pricking my ears up, and then return to the woman across the table. If men are as loyal as their options, what does it feel like to watch a man's gaze return to your face again and again and again?

The Most Expensive Date I've Ever Been On

When I worked in the movie industry, flirting on the phone was a daily phenomenon. Rolling calls, confirming meetings, setting up auditions; my routine was punctuated by suggestive little conversations with women I'd never met.

I was still freshly hatched from college and reeled with the idea that I could pick up the phone and call someone 'darlin' or 'sweetheart' during an otherwise perfunctory exchange. It felt like foxhole romance. Two overworked assistants managing the tentacular tyranny of a cranky producer or agent, finding a quick minute's respite before the paperweights started flying and neck veins bulged again.

One of my boss's best friends was an agent who was also working with us on several different projects. In the course of the day it wasn't unusual to place 10 or more calls to his office, and so I wound up forming a close phone flirtation with his assistant L. In hindsight, I'm not sure why I was ever attracted to her. She was definitely smart and attractive and full of self-confidence, but those adjectives could just as reasonably be applied to a horse.

Her voice was loud and assertive. She spoke quickly and without lingering over uncertain details. She sounded almost asexual, and it was with a little jolt of surprise that our conversations came to an end with a dollop of casual affection. 'Thanks, hon.' 'Talk to you soon, sweetie.'

After a few months I asked her out. I was worried that I might have been running away with myself. Maybe I had taken something out of context or misread off-handed friendliness as something it wasn't. I wondered if I was wedging an irreparable wall of awkwardness into an important working relationship. But when I asked her to drinks she happily accepted.

The night we were supposed to meet, we both worked late

and she called to suggest we have dinner instead. When we were talking about where to go I mentioned a distaste for sushi, which she immediately picked up on. She loved sushi and was determined to teach me how to enjoy it properly. We agreed to meet at some sterile Beverly Hills sushi place that doesn't exist anymore. It was glowing white and had an enormous fish tank that was so blue it looked digitized.

I was broke. I had a small mountain of student loans to pay off and was barely making enough to pay rent. I had no idea how much she made but she worked for the biggest agency in town. I assumed she had to be doing much better than I was. Still, I didn't think twice about agreeing to the restaurant. My boss had business lunches there. I saw the receipts in our expense reports, sometimes as much as 400 dollars for lunch.

It was stupid, but I felt giddy, like a kid dressing up in his father's suit. I was having a date at the same place my boss went to close deals and argue for greenlights.

When we met outside the restaurant I knew I was immediately out of my element. I was wearing puffy jeans and a button down shirt from TJ Maxx that my mother had given me for my birthday. She was wearing a form-fitting skirt suit that I'd only seen women wear on television. She looked like Heather Locklear on Melrose Place. I felt like Skippy from Family Ties.

When we were seated, she ordered a sampling of almost everything from the menu, including two of the three kinds of sushi that were seasonal and didn't have any price next to them. This was when I started to realize things were going to end badly for me. I was trying to do the rough math of all the things she had ordered but it had flown by so fast and the menu was barely intelligible to me. Words like 'Uni' and 'Tobi-Tama' weren't a part of my 23-year-old vocabulary. I lived with three other men in a shabby two-bedroom apartment piled halfway to the ceiling with empty beer bottles. I spent $30 a week on food.

After we had ordered I stopped caring about the bill. I was

excited about eating something new. There wasn't any romance between us, it was obvious from the first minute. We talked almost the whole time, but there was a dryness to it all. It felt like we were both trying to make the best of an evening that neither of us was enthused about continuing.

Just as the waiter brought the check, L got up and went to the restroom. I had planned to pay the whole time, but watching her excuse herself right at that moment I suddenly felt ridiculous, used. Not only did the date suck and the mysterious luster of our flirtations had been irrevocably lost, but now I was stuck with $150 bill for a bunch of briny rice balls.

I learned two things that night. Don't ever invite a woman to dinner unless you really care about her. More importantly, I really like sea urchin.

Women at Thirty, or the Scent of the Medicine Cabinet

When I turned 30 I threw myself a big party. I convinced a bunch of friends to come to Los Angeles for the weekend and hosted a big slumber party for two nights. Sleeping bags took over the living room floor and my bedroom was filled with everyone's luggage. I was worried about turning 30 for a long time. I was 25 when I abandoned my career in the movies to join Peace Corps. I was almost 29 when I finally returned. I had to start my life over from scratch. I did odd jobs for a few months before settling into a job testing video games with a bunch of high school students earning $290 a week.

Most of my college friends had made formal moves out of the squalor phase of their lives. They were lawyers, geologists, teachers, and homeowners. I wasn't worried about turning 30 because I felt old or decrepit, but I was aware that I'd sacrificed any real vertical achievement for the sake or a series of barely connected horizontal ambles. At 29 I was driving my father's 1994 Geo Metro and putting three weeks of my monthly salary toward rent.

The longer I thought about it, the more I realized that I didn't care. I was doing what I wanted to be doing; there was nowhere else I could have imagined myself. I wasn't exactly winning the fight, but I was engaged in one that I wanted to be fighting. When I realized that, I decided that I had something to celebrate.

This was also around the time I started seeing a 37-year-old woman. I thought about our age difference all the time. She graduated from college the same year I started high school. She never gave any outward signs of being uncomfortable with our age difference. I would make a point to avoid anything that drew attention to it. Every now and then she would reference her college days, or some high school stories and I would try and look straight through her, rapidly hitting the fast forward button in my mind.

I liked her. She was curious, giving, spontaneous, she had a pink streak in her hair and good taste in shoes. We got along well, and entertained each other with our differences. It was a great friendship with sex thrown in as a perk. Still, it was strange confronting the edge of a generation gap. Her favorite music seemed outmoded to me, and she spent money in a way that I had only seen in middle-aged housewives or children of privilege.

When we kissed her taste was neutral. There was no lingering musk, no trace of the fecund sex hormones flowing through her body. Her saliva tasted literal, perfunctory, not suggestive. Her neck always smelled of perfume, but there was a twinge of the medicine cabinet underneath. The bottoms of her feet were flattened and permanently callused the way my mother's feet were. She had the same white sunspots and thick knotty calves I'd seen on my mother growing up.

I don't know if my reaction had more to do with the fact that we were better suited as friends than lovers, but I sensed her age in everything. Even when I wasn't thinking about it directly, the age difference hung between us.

My friend S once told me about the joy her husband sometimes takes in trapping her under covers in a cloud of his flatulence. If I could one day learn to live with the stench of my lover's shit, I'm certain that a waft of the pill box on the nape would be manageable.

In retrospect, her age hung between us because there was a lot of distance between us to hang things in.

A few months later I slept with a 22-year-old. I wonder what I tasted like to her? I wonder how I smelled for her? Was there the germ of grandfather's old A-shirts in my sweat? Did my mouth have the beginnings staleness, of an old man gone a few too many hours without eating?

Sex is a window of opportunity. The farther apart your ages, the less incentive there is to go through that window together. You have to be in love with someone to make up for it, or else it becomes stilted and ghastly. When I turned 30, I realized that my own window had shifted. But I wasn't ready to let it shift that far ahead. Not without a better reason than being 'good friends.'

Get Your Hands Off of My Woman

There's something deeply territorial about being in a relationship. I went out to a bar with N one night and left her alone for a moment to go to the bathroom. When I came back there was a tubby guy in his late 30s sitting in my seat trying to make conversation with her.

The guy wasn't an enticing specimen. He had a desperate tinge to his laugh and he was dressed in Mom jeans and a dumpy jacket that fit him like a trash bag. Still, I felt a cockishness in the back of my brain. Who is this doughy little weasel that snuck into our corner booth the minute I got up? I crossed in front of him and took my seat, trying to politely follow what they were talking about.

I remember making sure to not show any territorial demonstrations of being with N. I forced myself to not put my arm around her, or rest my hand on her thigh. I wanted to show him that I wasn't threatened by his presence. I was lying to myself.

When I was 14, my older brother broke up with his girlfriend and called another girl he had dated to assuage his limping ego. She had started seeing someone new and after some contentious teenage words my brother wound up on the phone with her new boyfriend. They threatened each other for a few minutes and agreed to meet the following night to fight.

The next night, four kids rang our doorbell. They were hulking boys, not quite men, but strong enough to make the difference seem arbitrary. They were country boys, four junior firefighters in tank tops that showed off their veiny biceps and lumpy forearms. My brother went out to the front yard alone to talk to them. After some nose-to-nose man-barking one of them hit my brother in the face.

Seeing the three others waiting behind their friend, my brother turned around and started moving back to our front door. The kid jumped on his back and kept hitting him from behind. It looked absurd for a few seconds. Two grown men in a piggyback ride, arms and elbows flailing sloppily.

My brother threw the kid off his back and made it to the front door when my dad stepped in front of the boy. My dad is a bony accounting professor. He has a funny Danish accent and I've never seen him angry. He's not a fighter and when he stepped in front of the other boy it wasn't in aggression. But seeing my brother disappear in the front door the four kids turned on my dad. They surrounded him and let punches fly in a flurry. I heard the sick thud of bone and flesh smacking at high speed.

I saw my dad put an arm up to try and buffer the blows. He dropped to one knee. 'Stay down, old man,' I remember one of them saying as he stood above him. I had been watching the whole thing, too scared to move. They broke my dad's cheek and eye socket. He had blood in his eye for a month after.

Relationships can seem like an answer to some pervasive question; the elliptical dots at the end of all our metaphysical uncertainty. We idealize them as conclusions, irrevocable affirmations that we can be worthy and desirable partners. But relationships are as temporary and vulnerable as anything else. They are a long series of choices; everyday your partner must wake up beside you and decide that you're still what they want. Every night they must look around them and choose to come home to you in spite of all the other available choices.

It's easy in the beginning, when the love feels revelatory and the gravity of a new body is strongest. Over time, it's much harder to keep both partners mutually interested in fighting for one another, choosing to stay together with each passing day. We've invented convenient institutions to ameliorate the fear of being left, mandating the irreversible dictum of 'until death do us part.'

Knowing that you could promise away so much of your life to someone who could still walk away is scary. After all the dew-eyed promises and sincere vows of the ever after, there's no way to speak for tomorrow. You can't ever say what will happen. Sometimes it's enough to make a man hit another person. More than once.

Don't Google 'Fisting', and Why Women Apologize So Much

I have a weak constitution for some things. I've felt pretty comfortable believing there was little left in the world that could legitimately disgust me (save toenail fungus, which is a terrible thing). I thought of fisting as something so surreal and abstract it couldn't possibly elicit disgust.

The first time I saw the act performed was in a porn magazine one of my college roommates had (why does porn seem to self-replicate in boys' dorm rooms in college, owned by no one in particular?). It was entirely anticlimactic. Two tiny lesbians were stuck in freeze frame licking each other on a couch beside a fireplace, and in one of the frames, the tiny brunette had apparently slipped her hand into the blonde's vagina up to the wrist. 'So it is possible,' I thought. It didn't look all that bad. I'm sure that for a professional it's not an Olympic feat to accommodate the squished hand of an emaciated porn actress into their bodies for an extra few hundred dollars.

Years later, I was working for a talent management company in Beverly Hills and one of my co-workers called me over to his computer to watch something that a few of the other guys were marveling at in disbelief. At his desk I saw a brief video called 'Ass Tulip,' in which an actress had her anus fisted by a beefy man, and afterwards, through some horrible capacity of the human body pushed to its mechanical extreme, she was able to flex her butt in a way that made it flip inside out. This is the most nauseating thing I've ever seen. I feel a nauseous tickling in my nose just trying to describe it.

I always thought of fisting as a male perversion. It seemed motivated by a kind of arithmetic thinking that more is always better; something only a man could come up with. I remember the first time I put my hands down a girl's pants and realized I could actually fit a third finger into her vagina. I suddenly began to worry that she might think I was a novice for having only used two fingers for so long. I was totally surprised when she wriggled away after a minute. 'Ummmmm, I think three fingers is too many.'

I was even more surprised to learn that one of my friends has actually been fisted, and not just in the singular, past tense. It was actually a desired and enjoyable part of her sex life for quite a long time. Her girlfriend didn't have Neanderthal hands so this wasn't quite the mind-flipping carnival sideshow rendition of an internet image search might bring forth. It was something intense and deeply intimate, built up to over the course of several years together with her partner.

I once read a story on a sex blog called Single-ish, which Glamour publishes, about women who apologize too much. It described a night out at a bar playing pool with two men who felt compelled to give counsel to the helpless women trying to figure out which balls went where. The author described how her immediate reaction to missing a shot was to apologize to her male pedagogues.

The author would probably balk at the idea of her folksy musing being joined with fisting, but the two appeared almost one after the other on my computer. Some people are willing to make freakshows of their lives and bodies. Some people live in hygienically manicured bubbles where the use of the word 'darn' affords the luxury of alluding to something ugly without having to openly say it. Some people stick up for themselves and others flirt with physical ruin for the sake of testing their limits.

I have no interest in ever fisting somebody. The act of writing about it is enough to make me turn my head from the monitor and squint. But then I wonder: maybe there are some women in the world with vaginas that require a fist? Like the mythical micro-penis, perhaps there is an equal and opposite analog in women, the macro-vagina. Could I ever fall in love with someone that had a macro-vagina?

My Friend's Girlfriend is My Girlfriend

When I lived in Los Angeles, I would sometimes hook up with a woman my friend P had introduced me. They had dated the previous summer. She had just moved to LA and he thought she might need a friend in town.

During the few months that we were hooking up, I used to torture myself with the idea of her meeting my roommate. We were a bad match romantically, but I still swept myself away on a stream of admiration for her. She was as smart as anyone I've ever known, with an advanced math degree from a renowned university. Her fingers were always moving when she talked, opening and closing around some unseen shape.

She had droopy eyes that made her look perpetually drunk, and she drank heavily. She was cheerful and always welcoming; she had a habit of bringing random people from the street back to her house for parties after bars closed. Her living room was a patchwork cantina of Ivy League wine snobs, debauched beach bums, and whoever happened to be passing by on the street outside. In the middle of that she could still turn and look me in the eye and say something alarmingly direct and unflinching.

The first night we met, she hosted a small dinner party, then we went out to a bar in Santa Monica. She spent half the night in the bathroom crying over an ex-boyfriend. I remember standing next to some other guy who she had slept with a week earlier, trying to figure out what was wrong. He had an exaggerated afro-poof of hair and a strong jaw line with a dimple at the end. He quoted the lyrics to Peaches songs for the group and would then wait for us to share in his delight.

I imagined her looking at us leaning against the bar in the gaudy pinky light and bursting into tears, wishing her real man was there with her. Her private disappointments and public outbursts of joy made her seem reckless, both needy and self-sufficient. I was smitten.

I liked her more than she liked me. It was never going to work, it would never be more than a series of drunken interludes. My roommate was my opposite in all the ways that made me weakest and most prone to failure with her. He was loud and arrogant and full of caveman bravura. I secretly worried about bringing her around for fear that he would seduce her and then throw her out the next morning like an empty beer bottle.

A year later I was in San Francisco and they met at some group outing. They hooked up that night and they're still together. I was excited to learn that they'd hooked up once I could subtract my wet emotions from the equation. They're a good match and I hope they'll keep finding ways to be good to each other.

I've met a lot of the women that I've wound up sleeping with through friends. It makes sense that there would be a natural crossover for friends and girlfriends in a group of people who already have a strong affinity for one another. But we're not supposed to date people our friends have dated. It's off-limits; we're supposed to ignore innate attractions out of deference and loyalty.

I've slept with four women who had dated friends either before or after. Sex makes people vulnerable. You can't hide yourself when you're naked with someone, and it can feel like a betrayal when someone you've been naked with leaves you and gets naked with one of your best friends. Bros before hos, I was told during college.

My hos are my bros too, neither deserves a place above the other. And I wouldn't care about either if they asked me to avoid having new experiences, to protect their egos and insecurities. I'd rather just sleep with their ex-girlfriends. And I'm sure one day they'll be sleeping with more of mine.

Getting Laid

I haven't fact checked this idea, but I think there are more euphemisms for sex than for any other word in the English language. Many of them are cheap puns that help soften animal mysteries of sex. The more carried away with arousal and affection a person becomes, the more irrationally transcendent everything seems, sweating, breathing like a galloping horse, and swiveling hips to some erratic and primal rhythm. It is definitely not a thing that someone 'gets,' like finding a 20 dollar bill between the sofa cushions.

During her last week in San Francisco N asked me to come over after work one night to help her move some old furniture out of her apartment. As I was trying to negotiate the small puzzle of hallway, doorframe, and an ungainly couch, she said, 'I'm pretty sure you're going to get laid tonight for all the trouble.' 'I'm pretty sure that was going to happen regardless of moving the couch,' I told her.

At my worst, I'm prone to improvising sanctimonious sermons (did you know that?) about the terms people use around me. A flirting phrase of affection can, through my prism of logic, become grounds for a quasi-legal discourse about the etymologies of sexuality. I had never heard her use that phrase with me before, and I hadn't yet expounded on my deep loathing for the implied passivity and possession contained therein. Sex is not something you get, it's something you already have, which you agree to share with someone. I don't get vagina; it's not a status symbol waiting to be unwrapped and embraced like a new toy under the Christmas tree.

The 'laid' part doesn't do much for me either. It makes me think that I'm going to wind up flat on my back with sex miraculously happening to me while I watch in a comfortable recline. It makes sex seem like getting a massage. The implication is that there is a possessor of this mystical 'sex' and a person is lucky to find himself or herself in the passive role of the receiver.

It reaffirms the overbearing necessity of the man to always be the pursuer, foraging for sex like a bear in a thawing wasteland trying to find berries. Men are taught to celebrate their ability to get sex, to demonstrate their prowess to their peers based on the volume of their encounters. Men don't talk about the qualitative experiences with sex, only the underlying arithmetic that can be used as competitive leverage. Blowjob? Check. Doggy style? Check. Titty fuck? Check. Facial finisher? Check. Got 'em all. I'm that good.

Hauling the couch down the rectangular staircase, trying to keep from knocking all the pictures off the wall, I kept chewing on the phrase. I gnawed at it, wondering if I shouldn't pipe up about all the ugly images it connoted for me. I felt slighted almost. That wasn't the kind of sex we had ever had, and if it was going to start being that way, then I didn't want it.

When I was in high school, I remember raising my hand in English class to answer an open-ended question about something we had been reading. I don't remember what we were talking about or what point I wanted to make, but I remember the feeling of smug urgency emanating from inside. When I finished my ramble, my teacher looked at me for a second. He jutted his chin out and furrowed his brow, then turned away and walked to the center of the class. 'You know, Mike, if you were half as smart as you think you are, that would really be something.'

When I got the couch to the curb my jaw loosened, and I let all the flustered thoughts of indignation fall down. Those were mine; they existed in my head, and weren't transported there by the words she had told me. It would have been an argument with myself to protest any further.

It makes me a little sad now, to think that I had the momentary impulse to contort her words for my own subjective reasons just to make a point. It was a small thing, probably not even worth remembering, but those small choices are the ones that form behavior patterns in relationships. We choose what's acceptable and not acceptable to ask our partners to put up with. It becomes easier and easier to expect them to shoulder the brunt of our worst tendencies as a relationship ages.

This is part of what I fear most about being in a long-term relationship. I don't want to become someone cruel, but I'm afraid I'll lose the ability to separate my best self from my worst self in the rhetorical fog. In the end, every relationship becomes a fight with yourself.

We walked back upstairs together and looked at the new empty space in her living room. I grabbed my bag and put on my jacket. We walked back downstairs, found somewhere to eat, then we went to my apartment and had sex until three in the morning, until it was so late I had to stop because I had work in the morning.

We should have stayed up all night. The sleep wasn't worth it.

If You Can Get Me Hard I'll Show You A Good Time

One of the many things wrong with my earlier argument about why women suck in bed is the assignment of a gender stereotype based on an incomplete series of experiences. I've never had sex with a man, so I've never really considered that a lot of women might have similarly dispassionate experiences with passive men. Earlier this year, I found myself having sex in the same room as my friend A. I remember looking over periodically, seeing him draped on top of his date in a Romanesque recline. He looked like he was idling away an afternoon on one elbow, nibbling grapes out of a bowl with his mouth.

He and his date were still mostly clothed and making subtle head movements that looked tender and sweet. What looked like a coy moment of prom-night hesitation on the threshold of sex was actually water being tread to make up for the lack of an erection. At one point, after they had spent an hour kissing A said, 'If you can get me hard, I'll show you a good time.'

It was a sad little gauntlet being thrown down. We can have sex if you're willing to do the heavy lifting.

A word about A, before you get out the torches and pitchforks: he's a disaster of a man, but a lovely one. The first time we met he farted loudly and without apology, as if flatulating were a kind of greeting. He's also a spectacular alcoholic. I booze a lot, but A is a drinker in excess of my understanding of alcohol intake. He drinks so much his doctor gave him an Adderall prescription so he could concentrate in his grad school classes in spite of his hangovers. I can't think of a time when he hasn't been wearing something with a hole in it. At a friend's wedding he wore a pair of shoes someone had found in a public trashcan and given him as a joke. He laughed and then put the shoes on.

If I didn't know A, I would be inclined to write about how

men are acculturated to treat sex as an acquisition. The ideal scenario is for this man to smugly put his arms behind his head and watch his subject blow him, then ride him, then curl up in the crook of his shoulder and fall asleep in cartoonish exhaustion.

A is not that stereotype, even if I might have described him in a way to support that conclusion. Nobody is that gender stereotype. I got that wrong before. Sex is a communal activity, sometimes you wind up in close quarters with someone you thought you would want to share with, but at the close range you realize your assumptions were wrong. You have less to give them than you thought, there's nothing to say.

I've been in A's position before, with someone I didn't want to be with but didn't realize until it was too late. I faked it. I went through the motions begrudgingly. I lied. I blamed the fart on someone else, explained it away as some weak spot that other people have, but isn't a part of me.

A never got hard that night. He was too drunk and hopped up on pills; in a bed he didn't want to be in, with a person he would feel bad about having disappointed in the morning.

How I Would Make Love to Gloria Swanson

I once saw a delightful picture of wrinkled and saggy Helen Mirren splashing around in the ocean in one of the mystical beaches where celebrities go to be photographed by paparazzi. Helen Mirren is a beautiful woman, and seeing her disrobed at an age when sexuality is generally considered unappealing, made me smile. Of all the cultural fairytales we tell each other, the idea that sex between older people is somehow inferior to the nubile strains of the 20-something frightens me most. I can imagine at least a dozen younger celebrities more appealing than the aged Helen Mirren, but I don't know if I'd rather sleep with any of them.

Sex in America is the insinuating curves in perfume ads and the conveniently covered nipple on the cover of Maxim. It's the clown-faced pantomime of Samantha on Sex & the City, a performance done for the camera, whose lingering presence makes us feel more desirable. Physical symmetry is the social marching order; we must seek these well-aligned people out, assimilate to their styles and comportment in magazines and on TV, then feel grateful we've found someone young enough and symmetrical enough to inspire envy. Who would envy someone walking around with a slinky 61-year-old on their arm? Who could even stomach the thought of a 61-year-old in the act of ecstasy?

I watched Sunset Boulevard last weekend and was reminded of a theoretical flesh crawl with an older woman. Gloria Swanson is beautiful in that movie. Her role is a demented loon whose romantic attachment to William Holden is buffoonish, like some kind of ghoul parading around the land of young attractive people without any sense of shame. Her character's tragic flaw is that she can't accept her own age; she refuses to trade the indulgent vanities of her youth for something more age-appropriate. The way Gloria Swanson plays the role, clawing at her surroundings with wide-eyed delusion, is extraordinary.

The part of Norma Desmond is insane, but the woman playing the role is dashing. Watching Gloria Swanson act circles around a slack-jawed William Holden, I felt charmed. When she slipped her arm through his while watching her old movies in the living room, I felt a jealous tingle on my leg. William Holden squirmed with discomfort at the idea of a 50-year-old woman's advances. The opportunity was wasted on him. The things I would have done with that hand in my lap, sitting beside someone so alluringly capable and in command of themselves.

Is there an alternative for Norma Desmond that isn't a patronizing dismissal? Is there a way for her to lead a sane life without having to sacrifice her force and vivacity on some tubby butler? Do older people abdicate the right to be open about their physical and sexual needs because of the slackening of their skins and the onset of bunions? I hope not.

When I'm old I imagine my hunger for body and closeness will remain, even if my hard-on might have to go on meds to keep pace. I can see myself visiting my grown children, staying in the strange sheets of the guest room, listening to the eerie quiet of an unfamiliar neighborhood in a strange city. In that room I can imagine myself turning to my post-menopausal partner, taking her speckled hand, with its knots of blue-green veins, and putting it around the back of my head as I follow my salivary divining rod to that most indignant of all god's creations: the geriatric vagina. She sometimes looks like Gloria Swanson in my imagination.

Going to Bed Angry

The stupid thing about aphorisms is that I can never remember where I heard them first. At some point in my life someone told me that you're never supposed to go to bed angry in a relationship. It might have been a greeting card, a sitcom, or in a book I parsed through during a lazy summer. Now I've absorbed it as a subconscious truth without having ever really thought about it for myself. And there are plenty of times I've fallen asleep angry, lying next to someone I loved.

One time was in Madagascar. I spent my two years there orbiting around in an unrequited love for T. Toward the end, things had reached a sad point of strain. I was coming to understand the myriad reasons things hadn't worked out between us. I was withdrawing. The closer we got to the end, the further I withdrew. I tried to let my emotional investment in her fall away.

Seeing her those last months reminded me of the loneliness at the pit of my bowels. I still loved her but I realized I didn't fit in her life in the way I wanted. I would make a point to sit with other people the few nights we were in the capital together during our final departure conference. One of the last nights together was in the Peace Corps flop, crammed into a twin mattress in the top bunk of a room shared with six other people. We fell asleep back-to-back. I didn't know why we were even sharing a bed. It seemed like a structural formality, or a social obligation since beds were in short supply.

I had a terrible nightmare that night. I dreamt I was walking through a bright and sandy village with lots of roadside stands made of bamboo and palm fronds. I walked through some huts and wound up in a dugout canoe with a Malagasy person oaring me down a rivulet, steering away from the ocean. T was in another canoe heading in the same direction. My friend M was in the canoe with her. M was seeing T's best friend and had a natural friendship with T, free of all the weighted angst that dragged on all of our interactions. They were looking away from me.

T and M kept moving steadily onward while my canoe began to drift behind. I watched them move further away from me.

I woke up with a sharp inhale, sweating intensely, filled with sadness. It was almost 4AM. In my sleep I had turned so that I was looking at T's back in the darkness. My heart was beating fast and my brain felt like a gyroscope rotating on a wobbly axis. I turned back onto my side so my back would be to T.

I heard T exhale behind me. I felt the mattress shift as she turned over. I couldn't tell if I had woken her or if she was still sleeping. She pressed her torso into my back and reached across my shoulders and chest. I put my hand on her forearm. She exhaled loudly, like a vent. I was worried I was too sweaty in her arms and shifted away on my hip a few inches, but she pulled me back even closer and didn't let go.

I felt my brain slow down, her skin was familiar under my hand. It smelled like what was underneath all the perfume, scented soaps, and mango moisturizer that was her chemical trace. It was the unadorned version of herself, the smell of a body without an apologetic medium in between. She'd told me she loved me before, but I never believed her. She never acted like it, when she said it to me it sounded like an aphorism, like it was the next line in the script of our own private sitcom.

In the morning I told her I had had a nightmare and asked if I had woken her. She said she had slept the whole night through.

Don't go to bed angry. Or else do.

My First STD

A few years ago I got the first (and, so far, only) sexually transmitted disease of my life. I first noticed it toweling myself off after a shower. There were a bunch of little red pimples in my crotch. Uh oh, that's new.

I'm usually pretty conservative when it comes to sleeping with people. I'm typically diligent about condom use and avoiding hooking up with random strangers. The few one-nighters that have escalated all the way to sex have almost always been with someone that I knew before in some capacity or another. So, rightly or wrongly, I've always felt there was a subconscious barrier between STDs and my special little person. Hearing STD talk was like listening to my married friends debate mortgages and interest rates, they just weren't dimensionally applicable to me.

Whoops.

After consulting with the doctor I learned that I had something called molloscum contagiosum, an innocuous skin infection that doesn't have any major complications and usually heals itself if left untreated. Treatment isn't necessary but I got to go to the dermatologist anyway for a few rounds of punctures, scrapes, and cauterizing. Walking out of the doctor's office I felt both relieved and ashamed. I had subconsciously shifted demographic pools. I'm in the ho category now. Every questionnaire I fill out for the rest of my life will have to have the man-ho box checked with a big red X.

The next queasy task was calling the two people I had to inform of my trollop-itis. If ever there is a moment to put your tail between your legs it's calling someone you've hooked up with a month or two after the fact to tell them you've got an STD. I felt three inches tall with thimble-sized lungs incapable of holding in enough air, trying to explain what this daunting

Latinate malaise was. Imagine answering your phone on at work one morning and being told that you could have something in the 'contagiosum' family. How are you even supposed to broach the subject? Hey there, I know we haven't spoken in five or six weeks but I think you maybe gave me crotch pimples. And if not, then I might have given them to you. See you around.

After the queasiness wore off, the whole thing started to seem absurd. A fair majority of my friends have had an STD in some capacity or another. Warts, herpes, gonorrhea, even HIV. Before, I had listened to them recount the stories of how they came to expose themselves to these lurid little stocking stuffers gleefully. I realize it's perverse, but I felt I had achieved a new kind of closeness with them. It felt like I had lettered in STDs and could now jockishly strut around the hallways high-five'ing my pals on game day. This was all the more entertaining because, of all the STDs to catch, it seemed like I had gotten off with only the lightest of metaphysical reprieves.

It's strange to imagine all the life-altering potential in sex. From pregnancy to death, there's an amazing spectrum of change that can come out of it. There's the great absurdity in it, the huge chasm between what it feels like inside and what is actually going on outside.

I always wonder what some of my most intense sexual experiences would look like on tape. They would be ridiculously comic, like some gangly documentary on the mating habits of spider monkeys. It's mind-boggling to reconcile the mechanics of hip thrusting and bodily fluid exchange with the genuine intimacies of lovemaking. It's like a really bad joke in which our bodies are always the punchlines. That's why I find it so disconcerting to see all those hyper-real images of sex and seduction everywhere. It's like advertising internet service with lots of soft focus pictures of fiber optic cables; as if the vessel had anything to do with the experience contained within.

It's easy to become hypnotized with sexuality. It feels great, and we're surrounded on all sides by pressures that encourage us to go out and hump one another like some surrogate form of retail therapy. And then there's the hormonal urgency of nature. If there is a god, I imagine watching us conduct our sexual lives is its version of YouTube. I can see god opening the link and watching with peels of laughter the clip where I get molloscum in some drunk and delusional state of ecstasy. It's funny.

Show Me Your Penis

It's stupid that there aren't more penises in movies. I see my own penis everyday, several times. There's nothing remarkable about it. I admit to looking at it with a fond eye sometimes, imbuing its sloping pink dangle with a certain nostalgia. Even still, genitals have somehow become danger signals to many people, giant red X's that can't be looked at without tearing the moral fabric of the universe.

Penises aren't any more or less attractive than vaginas. They can have unpleasant qualities, but in terms of visual appeal I'd say they're at least an order of magnitude more attractive than the average foot. Of course anyone can go barefoot, regardless of what calloused and veiny claws they might have, but penises need to be treated like a controlled substance. Though you might have one of your own, you must be of a certain age before you're allowed to see someone else's at the movies.

The videogame is not often cited as a figurehead of social progress, but the expansion for Grand Theft Auto IV, called 'The Lost and Damned', features a conspicuous penis appearance. Penises have appeared in games before, many of them, probably too many to recount. What's remarkable is that GTA IV is not a marginal or pornographic game. It's one of the biggest franchises in videogame history. Having a penis in GTA IV is like Harrison Ford showing his male rudder in an Indiana Jones movie.

There's nothing remotely interesting about the scene that the nudity is used in. It's filled with stereotype and cheap jokes about how gross the male genital is supposed to be. A corrupt politician, consciously delivering his orders while naked is an extension of the dick-centric machismo that 13 year-olds have been giggling about since time began. Dicks are disgusting, but the most powerful man in the room is so confident in his position that he is unaffected by the revulsion of his audience. Their reactions, for better or worse, are immaterial. Even if he doesn't literally have the biggest dick in the room, he's still aware that he's got the biggest figurative dick.

The punchline underscores how completely absurd all of those abstract phallocentricities are when taken literally. For an organ whose size is always a point of interest, it's absurd to come to the end of a three-minute scene only to see the flaccid, middle-aged, polygon appendage. A penis is always only a penis.

I still don't understand what's so shameful or disgusting about seeing a penis. I've met a lot of people who seem preprogrammed to scrunch up their faces and squint every time the subject arises. It's as if the existence of genitals were as repellent as boogers or cooties. The imperfections of the penis, the veins, the pubic hair, the alien skin of the scrotum, the suggestion of autonomous movement when it flexes; it's all cause for recoil.

Many men certainly have similar knee-jerk reactions to the image of the vagina. The vagina must be the mystical honey box from which all life flows, but further talk about menstruation, vaginal flatulence, or hairy labias are unwelcome.

If those discrepant anxieties exist, it seems like art would be the perfect place to exorcise them. In the same way that serial killers and heartless fascists armed with nuclear warheads dance around the flickering mobile of the film world, it's only natural that genital anxiety might be an undiscovered genre for story-tellers.

It's like we live in two different worlds: the anatomically safe one where gender is based on personality stereotype and facial features, and then a kinky underworld where the ugly grammatical points of our bodies rub against each other in the darkness. It's always surprising to me when I go into the bathroom at work and unzip my pants for a piss and don't see that dangerously unpredictable underworld come rushing out like the ghosts inside Pandora's box.

Instead, it's just another body part, a mistranslation, a lost remnant from a parallel universe where feelings don't have to be kept separate from the vessels that transport them.

Talking About Sex With Your Parents

My dad came to the city for an afternoon to help me mail some boxes the day before I moved to New York. As we were talking about times to meet, I mentioned I had an appointment for an HIV/STD test.

My dad was quiet for a second, then said 'Uh huh. Well, how about the next day then.'

I grew up in a religious home. My parents are Seventh-Day Adventists. My brother and I had to go to church every Saturday morning growing up. We had to observe the Sabbath too, which meant from sundown Friday until sundown Saturday we weren't allowed to watch TV or spend the night at our friends' houses. I took these restrictions as unavoidable inconveniences when I was a kid. When I was 16 I read the bible in its entirety and tried to believe in my parents' dogma. It didn't take so much. The more I read and thought about it, the less I believed.

By the time I left for college I was on my way to leaving their religious cocoon for good. Caffeine, alcohol, pork, and pre-marital sex all worked their way into my day-to-day life. I would happily debate the principles and rhetorical validity of religion, but with sex, I would almost never make reference to my own life. And my parents never showed any interest in learning more about my sex life.

It was taken for granted that I would avoid sex until marriage. I didn't want to go out of my way to be dishonest with them, but there weren't many occasions to bring up my sex life in the course of normal holiday conversation. It's not that I don't want to tell them. But I never feel like I have a reason to. I assume both of them were virgins until they married so I'm not sure how worthwhile it would be to have a conversation about having sex with my best friend's ex.

I don't want to hold that back from my parents. I don't have children so I'm not sure what it's like to cross the last border of sexual reckoning with a son or daughter. What is it like for a parent to reckon with their child's sex life, especially when it is based on such different choices from their own?

After my dad and I had dropped all my boxes off at the post office and finished the last round of errands for the move, he looked at me sideways and then looked down again. 'So when will you get the results of your test?' he asked.

'I got it back already,' I told him. 'They can do most of it on the spot now. It was all negative.'

'Mmmhmm,' he said.

He looked straight ahead, one hand on the steering wheel. I wondered when it was that he last had sex. I didn't ask.

The Hooker on the Corner

There was a hooker who worked on the corner in front of my building in San Francisco some nights. When I first moved in a little over a year ago, a couple of my guy friends drove up to visit me from out of town. As we headed inside after spending the night at a bar, she asked why we didn't have any women with us. 'Ain't no one gettin' laid if you go up there by yourselves,' she half-shouted after us. She sounded almost angry. She seemed insulted that we hadn't offered her to join us.

She hadn't said a word to me since that night. I didn't see her very often, but every few weeks she'd be out on the corner again, in short pants and high heels, walking with a friend or staring anxiously down the street. I lived on the third floor with a sliding glass door and warped balcony that looked out to sidewalk below. I'd leave my blinds open at night until right before going to bed because I liked the city lights and the way the buildings tuck away into shadows of Twin Peaks. I would see her down there some nights and watch her for a minute, forgetting that she could look back up and see me in the wide open glass door just as easily. But she would never look back up.

I'd seen her leaning into a car that's pulled up to the curb. Sometimes she would get in, other times the car would drive away and leave her shifting her weight from heel to heel. Sometimes she wouldn't be around for weeks at a time, and new girls in sequined strips of fabric and plastic heels would take her place. One night I was walking home from work after staying too late in the office and saw a man sitting in a parked car. His right arm was extended over the passenger seat and it looked like he was staring at the steering wheel. When I got closer I saw a woman's head pressed into his lap, just barely moving.

He looked at me and I immediately felt like I was trespassing. I turned away, staring down at my shoes. I didn't look back.

I used to work with someone who told me you pay the hooker to leave at the end, and it seemed so perfectly opaque that I thought it must have been a lie. I was still young and thought that there was some great secret to sex. It seemed like there was some private language to finding a partner. I could see it happening all around me but I still didn't understand the words.

When I had sex for the first time, I was 23. It was a delicious anti-climax. It was like a good shit crossed with an indulgent soak in a hot tub. I had romanticized things so hopelessly up until that point, I hadn't been able to discover how stupidly easy it is to find someone to have sex with. I thought there would be some elemental signpost drawing me to my missing half then something vaguely mystical would happen, like inadvertent levitation. I thought sex lay buried in some glyphic tomb of intimacy.

But no, it was just a body function in the end, a vessel that could be filled, but alone was an empty serving plate covered in garnishes. Once I got my sex legs beneath me I found out how strangely awful it can be to wake up with someone you don't want, to have their taste in your mouth, and their smell around your body. Sex was a cheap parlor trick when I didn't care about the person on the other side of the bed. As good as it was at the height, the drop back down to the morning after seemed to last so much longer.

When I see the hooker on my corner, she seems invincible. She walks with her back straight, she struts, she speaks loudly, yells at passersby when moved to do so. She seems strong and unbridled. She would have to be to spend so many nights being told to leave, over and over again.

Don't Make Poopy in the Office

I once went out drinking with some PR people after a media event I had to attend for work. I hate attending media events. It's like reporting on an infomercial, set in upscale hotel conference rooms or cold downtown discos. I had spent all day at one hotel trying to wring something interesting from the anemic presentations and smiling non-responses. As the sun went down I abandoned one hotel for another, this time ascending to a roof top bar for free hors d'oeuvres and information dissemination. As the event wound down I engaged myself in a conversation with a couple other writers and some PR people who entreated us to join them for drinks at a bar not affiliated with a hotel empire. It was a weeknight and I had lots of other work to get to at home, but I went along anyway.

PR people are a strange group, tasked primarily with crafting and controlling the message about a subject that they've had no hand in creating. They tend to be bright and motivated people, working long hours in a state of perpetual cheer. It's almost like metaphysical philanthropy, though the pay is certainly better. As a writer, I'm usually the primary target of PR people. All those toothy smiles and dainty pigs in a blanket on silver platters are intended for me. I get to be patronized on a regular basis by people in expensive clothes.

So it was probably a trick of delusion and free beer when my eyes settled on a manic blonde with a bob and a pug nose. This must be what it's like for women to see a man in uniform. At 10:30 at night she seemed like she was on a schedule, like she had somewhere to go, something to facilitate. I imagine my attraction to a woman like this, the kind I could reasonably imagine switching from tennis shoes to pumps just before walking into the office, is some cultural seed left over from my childhood. My formative years were spent in the 80's, ogling blondes on TV and in the movies. I was fixated on soap operas, Santa Barbara was my favorite. Between Helen Slater, Cybil Shepherd, and Marcy Walker my childhood passion for flouncy silk business shirts and women conquering male-dominated industries was set.

For the first 30 seconds or so, this woman completely fit that mold. I was on the verge of breaking off the conversation I was having, arguing very passionately about videogames, to try and talk to her. She hadn't acknowledged me in any way. It was my inner canine raising its wet nose and stiffening its ears. Then I pulled back on my leash. Hitting on someone in front of an audience of colleagues, someone I'll likely have to work with in the future, is probably the worst of all the three-beer ideas I've ever had.

It's easy to create work crushes. Spending so much of your waking life moving in a contained population, in an office or an insular industry, it's hard not to gravitate to those that stand out against the background noise. It's tantalizing to take a few disconnected qualities and project a whole person onto them, and then sweep yourself away with a wispy idea. An upturned nose, a blonde bob, a black business skirt. Someone catch me before I fall.

The F U Date

I met M at a dirty bar decorated with large oil paintings of small breed dogs winsomely staring from their frames. She was animated with a casual mania, dressed in tight black pants and thrift store boots. I had worked late and rushed to the bar to avoid being too late. We arranged to meet at 9:30. I showed up at 10, riding on a wave of apologetic texts. M was outside waiting for me. We hugged and walked inside. She looked like a teenage boy in drag, like one of the dimpled kids I imagine might have dawned a wig and played Ophelia in the 17th century.

We settled into a booth pressed against one of the front windows. M spoke in a soft voice. I kept asking her to repeat herself, leaning in to better hear her. She spoke quickly but would slow down at the end of her sentences and punctuate her thoughts with a widening of her eyes. She disoriented me. I felt like I was watching a hummingbird hovering in mid-air, the rapid flapping of its wings almost imperceptible in the surrounding calm.

I mistrusted everything she was saying. I felt like she was trying to hypnotize me with ornamental motion and a kind of mystic explication of David Lynch movies. I noticed she wasn't opening her mouth much as she spoke. I started to catch glimpses of flickering metal in between her lips. 'Do you have braces?' I asked.

She immediately pursed her lips and looked away blushing. 'Yeah,' she said.

I asked her to show me her braces. She didn't want to, but I pressed her. Seeing braces in the mouth of a 28-year-old woman was immediately more exciting to me than hearing more armchair philosophy about film. I had braces when I was in my early 20s so I felt a basic kinship with her handi-capable mouth. The more reassuring I tried to be the more she shied away from showing me.

I realized I was being too nice to her. I knew as soon as I saw her that we didn't have a strong connection, and the more we talked the more I realized that we weren't a good match. I'm blunt, deliberate, and invasive. She was effervescent and insinuating, filled with a self-possessed mystery that I could never have taken seriously. But the fact that her teeth were literally strapped into a metal stricture so commonly linked to the embarrassment of puberty was exciting. I had gone through that as an adult too. I wanted to share that with her.

My friend C insists the first time we met I told her to fuck off. We were sitting on a plane from Beijing to Chengdu and I was sulking in my window seat looking at the stepped rice patties cut into the gorges below. She introduced herself and told me about some mixtape her girlfriend had made her, then let me listen to one of the songs from it. After three minutes trying to separate Tori Amos from the roar of jet engines I handed back her earbuds. I asked if she ever had the experience of being unable to say anything in English after having been in a foreign country for a long period of time.

She said she hadn't and quickly moved back to another conversation she had been having across the aisle. I didn't have anything to say about her Tori Amos song, but was feeling honestly overwhelmed with Chinese culture shock. She took it as a personal sleight against her personal confession, and spent the next several days stewing over how I had offended her. She retaliated by embarking on a small crusade to get me to like her.

Watching M squirm, I realized I was being too nice to her. Did she really want some guy to validate her discomfort with metal fixtures in her mouth? Was the sea change in my personality, going from half-hearted engagement in a chat about movies to fixated curiosity about something completely superficial, too much to handle?

We all like having our insecure parts teased. It's a kind of intimacy when someone can look at you, spot your weakest area, and tickle it with some well-placed movement. There's an exhilaration at having been discovered. The subconscious nakedness of it can help cement a link between two people sharing a common frame of reference.

Conversely, there's something distancing about someone who wants to only validate the people around them. (N called me a 'yes man' once, which I took painfully, wincingly, because with her it was true.) Showering someone with attention, insinuated promises of kindness and understanding, is always self-reflexive. It doesn't point to any genuine understanding of the other person, but is a kind of self-aggrandizing act of generosity. It's less sharing and more taking.

When M finally relented and gave me a few seconds of a wide-mouthed smile, showing off her parallel rows of metal, I was only thinking of myself. That's what I must have looked like when I was 22 and eating sushi with L, or asking bartenders to make anything so long as it was blue. I didn't like M enough to tell her to fuck off. Instead, we talked about David Lynch and Miranda July. Then we kissed for a while.

Close to midnight I walked her back to her bike. We said goodbye and I watched her flit away into the night, like some flannel appointed hummingbird. I'm pretty sure I'll never see her again.

Having Sex on Inauguration Night

Pictures are liars because of us. They trap a moving, changing moment into a single frame that points to a vague encapsulation of the truth. I saw a picture of Barack and Michele Obama dancing face to face at the inaugural ball, and I immediately started wondering if they were going to have sex that night. I wonder what it must be like to be so close to a lifemate after having gone through such a major transformation, from gangly law student to American figurehead. Does sex have a place in that world anymore? Is there time for physical intimacy with so many dire threads dangling on the periphery of the celebration?

Watching someone evolve is inevitable in relationships. This is very often a bad thing, a kind of gradual slackening. Getting married is a finish line, a celebratory goal after which two people give over to the pursuits of property management, consumption, and an annual vacation to a postcard somewhere in South Western Bavaria or the West Indies. How many people get to see their partners actually excel over time? How many loving spouses watch their mate become more than he or she was as an awkward undergrad?

It's hard not to see the sex between them, watching the Obama's dancing against a blue sea of heads gazing up in the darkness. Barack's forward-leaning posture, his chin jutting hungrily into Michelle's face, I can almost see the thoughts in his head. The wetness, the warm touching of skin, the rhythmic thrust inward, straining to ascend, the hips rising in anticipation of his momentum. The arch up, the coming together, the falling back, the dilated pupils, the clenched hands, fingers interlocked.

It all becomes a metaphor in the picture when I look at it, the two people there project sexual silhouettes, stuck in the gaze of a political machine, but still holding onto the mundane mystery of a human relationship.

One of my greatest fears about long-term relationships is thinking about the ways that I'll change over time. I don't feel any different inside now than I did when I was a boy, but pictures tell me that I have changed. I can only imagine what changes are left for me in the coming decades. This image terrifies me: a woman looking at me in 20 years, wondering where the wave broke, wondering when the man I used to be transformed into the slouching, wrinkled reduction sitting on the couch.

It makes me woozy to imagine a relationship that is still on the upslope 20 years later, cresting unimagined territory, moving forward in tandem. I can't imagine experiencing it from that height without needing the expression of affection to take a physical form, to put in primal action all the things words miss.

But it's just a picture in the end. A stolen frame, a fraction of a second in a night that must also be larded with hand shaking, obsequious coddling, political ingratiation, and impersonal pomp. How much of that momentary flush of desire can be left after a maelstrom of toothy smiles and flashing bulbs? I don't know. When I imagine myself in that position, the secret service is guarding the door while I'm in the bathroom fucking my wife, trying to hold on, in momentary freefall.

Kissing in the Rain

I met M off Market Street just after sunset. She was studying in a coffee shop and I saw her through the window while I was still talking to her on the phone. We walked up to Chinatown to a bar I'd gone by lots but never been inside.

It was bright and empty when we got there. We sat in a booth in the back, lined with red vinyl. It was a Friday night and it had been a long week for me. I was tired and felt my whole body relax happily after the first few sips of my drink. I was drinking bourbon and soda. I inherited this habit from N. I used to drink Old Fashioneds, Manhattans, or Harvey Wallbangers. After she left I started ordering bourbon and soda as if it were some kind of psychic howl, a broken show of solidarity to no one but myself.

We made small talk for an hour. I explained my job and my time in Peace Corps, the two conversational constants of almost every date I've ever been on in the last several years. She talked about grad school, some time spent in Japan, disappointment in having traded New York for suburban California. A loud group sat in the booth next to ours and we made fun of them for a while, we took turns exploring the basement, where the bathrooms were, just beyond a disco floor lying dormant, waiting for more people to arrive.

I couldn't tell if M was attracted to me. We were talking comfortably but it wasn't flirtatious. I remember her casually dropping the term 'normative' into our conversation, and that was enough for me. I was smitten, at least momentarily. I left my arm up on the edge of the booth when she went to the bathroom. I told her she was pretty when she came back. 'Thank you,' she said, and looked into her lap.

After a couple of hours of conversation, M had to leave to catch her train out of the city. It was a mile and a half walk back to the train station. While we were walking through the backend of Union Square it started raining. I tried to hail a cab for us, but they all sped past us in the rain.

We kept walking. I put my arm around her and pulled her closer to me. I wanted to kiss her. We kept missing red lights at every intersection so there was no natural excuse to stop walking. I thought about stopping mid-block and kissing her against the glass wall of a department store. It made me feel self-conscious, we were still talking fast enough and it would have felt abrupt. It made me nervous.

Somewhere south of Market I saw the light ahead of us change to yellow as we were approaching. We came to a stop in front of the red light. I waited for her to finish what she was saying, forcing myself to not respond. When the pause came, I put my hand on her check and tilted her head towards mine. We kissed for a minute or so, our clothes wet, my glasses beading with rain. We caught another red light at the next block and kissed again.

After another minute she pulled away. This was the last train of the night, and she was getting closer and closer to missing it.

When we got to the station it looked empty and the glass doors were closed. There was a janitor inside mopping the floor. He told us the last train had just left for the night. She called a friend from school and arranged to stay with him for the night. We took one of the cabs waiting in front of the station to his neighborhood and said goodnight.

Then the loud music kicked in and the credits rolled up the screen.

Let's Just Be Friends

I was talking to my friend S one night who wondered why I don't write more about some of my women friends who have been so ridiculously important to me. 'Well,' I thought, 'what does friendship have to do with dating?' Then I remembered the two hours I had spent on the phone with S a few days after I had met N. I was seconds from sending her a wedding proposal in a text message. We'd only spend a day together at that point, but I was beyond reason, at the point of emotional submersion where there is no way to tell up from down. Without S's patient ear I might have engineered a small catastrophe, like a puppy dog run amok during high tea.

I don't know what separates an intimate friend from a lover. S has seen all of my nasty, ugly bits: the weakness, the pettiness, the callousness, the immaturity. With people I'm seeing there's always a pressure to keep myself together. I always feel attenuated to how the another person is perceiving me. It's absurd, admittedly. I have no idea what I look like and feel like to the person looking back at me, but I'm always conscious of their look and want to do what I can to impart it with attraction and affection. With S, I don't feel pressure to be anything other than myself. I probably respond by overcompensating with my crass and vulgar sides (the number of times she must have heard the term 'bukkake' in our phone conversations; sigh).

S was recently told me something astounding about knowing she was ready to commit the rest of her life to her husband. 'I've not wanted to have sex with that man,' she said. 'If he were ever in a position where he became physically incapable, I would literally wipe his butt for him. I would be okay with that.' I become fatalistic and irrationally swept away in romance. Hearing S talk about love in such blunt terms, acknowledging the transient nature of all of those cues of attraction and infatuation we so easily mistake for love was totally stunning. Perhaps those observations might be obvious to the average person, but my self-involved ego was agog that the true measure of love might be fecal.

I remember one Thanksgiving my father had to excuse himself from the dinner table because my grandmother had shit herself while we were eating. She was old and mostly senile, living in a nursing home. He took her to the bathroom and helped her clean herself and changed her into new underwear. I had never seen love in such a literal state before. When you love someone things shift. My maternal grandfather was engaged to another woman when he met my grandmother. He had to break off the engagement and go against the wishes of his whole family and risk alienating most people in the tiny town where he lived to follow after the woman he loved.

Those two experiences have become the bookends of love for me. You begin with something so overwhelmingly life-affirming and beautiful that you risk the most basic foundations to make it work. And in the end, you're left with someone who can't remember their name and shits their pants when there's too much butter in the gravy.

I love S, but I don't know if I would clean up her shit. I probably would, but I would be angry about it and I would hold it over her for the rest of her life. Maybe that's the difference, finally. We don't resent our friends for not being willing to wipe up our shit after we've lost control. But in love, there is an unspoken expectation that the other person be ready to put up with your everything, from the cute quips to the tragic incontinence, and still look you in the eye and say that you're charming and lovable. Love is cruel and unfair in that way. It's a harrowing thing, and would probably be fatal were it not for friendship.

Here's to you S. I love you. May you never have to wipe my butt.

Infidelity

When I'm seeing someone new there are two ideas I use to torture myself about the other person. The first is that I imagine that the woman I'm seeing used to be a man and is secretly waiting for an opportune time to reveal this sensitive bit of post-op information to me. The second and more common idea is to imagine they're off sleeping with someone else on nights when we can't be together. I don't take either very seriously; both ideas pop up and evaporate again quickly after they've bubbled into my brain. The sex change notion is admittedly ridiculous. So is the fear of being cheated on, at the end of the day, but it seems to strike a much deeper chord.

I have never cheated on anyone. To the best of my knowledge, I've never been cheated on either. I'm not all that concerned with the idea of being cheated on. It's a superficial insecurity I have when I'm seeing someone. The idea looms when a call gets forwarded to voicemail some night I was hoping to come over: of course she can't answer the phone, she's busy thumping some random bartender from the corner dive bar. And he's probably got better abs than me, a bigger dick, and can hold out all night without coming.

The fear that your partner is cheating on you is almost always self-reflexive. It's a subconscious way to lacerate yourself with your private insecurities. To take these fears seriously is to admit, on some level, you've got less invested in your partner as a person than as salve for all of those psychic weak spots. Sex is a powerful and thing, but it's still driven by wants that are usually beyond our ability to rationalize. For all of its ascendant potential, its still base and animalistic, no more important than a glass of water as the Leninism goes.

There's a certain evolutionary logic to the fear of infidelity. I'm sure proto-man's worst fear was the idea of someone else laying seed in his partner because it represented a direct threat to his lineage. I don't think I could ever begrudge a partner the fulfilling of some basic physical satisfaction. At the same time, we're not cave people anymore and the choice to enter into a monogamous relationship with someone and then double back on that promise is a loud indicator of something amiss.

I couldn't bring myself to masturbate for a month after N left. When I finally did I barely even felt the orgasm. I looked down at the opening on the tip of my penis as I was coming and it seemed like a sad little mouth wailing forth some fluid version of a whale song, mourning. The body, the form, and the function remain, but the special purpose had gone away. That's why the notion of cheating has never seriously occurred to me when I've been seeing someone I loved. I definitely register interest and attraction in other people, but there's such a gap between the gratification of a good fuck with a stranger and the kind of ecstatic experience of having sex with someone you love that it's not seriously comparable. If the form and function supercede the intimate purpose of the act, than there's probably an impasse in the way you relate to your partner.

Then again, I may be wrong. Thinking about the kinds of statistics that Peggy Vaughn popularized (60% of married men wind up having extra-marital sex, 40% of married women) I wonder what happens to that high-minded ideology after 20 years with the same person? Does sex with a long-term partner inevitably return to being a basic body function, the proverbial glass of water? If it does, should it matter if your partner gets their water from a different faucet from time to time?

Listening to the Neighbors Have Sex

I went to bed early one Friday night in San Francisco. I felt guilty for not doing more to inaugurate the weekend with something social, but I was exhausted. Thursday was our office holiday party and I was out too late, up too early the next morning, and bleary eyed by sundown. As I was brushing my teeth I heard some moaning coming through the walls of my apartment. I was immediately curious because my neighbor was an older woman, near 70, who lived alone. The idea of her having sex at 10:30 on a Friday night immediately tickled at my curiosity.

In the year and a half that I lived in that apartment I almost never heard anything from my neighbor. She'd crank the TV up when Dancing with the Stars was on, and I'd listened to some of her rambling diatribes on the subject when she caught me on the balcony some nights. She got visits from her son, who was the super for our building, and sometimes she'd babysit her new grandson. Otherwise her social life is entirely comprised of television and her overfed cat.

The idea that she had suddenly had enough, decided to put on some lipstick, walked out to the smokeless jazz bar on 25th Street and brought home some spot-bellied gentleman caller to listen to her vinyl collection was exciting. It's easy to take for granted the more basic physical needs of those around us. There is a fundamental shame about body function and nakedness that sits in perilous opposition to the idea of close-quarters living in an apartment building.

I used to feel an embarrassment some mornings when I walk to my dresser after showering and realize I was naked and in plain view of anyone on the sidewalk or in the building across the way. I was looking at some porn clips in between bouts of writer's block one night without realizing that the volume on my computer was turned all the way up. As the trumpeting cries of the actors came blaring from my speakers I literally jumped out of my seat.

My neighbor on the other side was a young and attractive woman who just moved to the city. I'd hear her talking on the phone some nights or else talking to her small terrier when he acted up. I was certain that this blast of truck-stop porn was coming through loud and clear on her side of the wall. What would she think of me the next morning as we passed each other in the hallway, me late for work and her on her way to walk the dog? She would see me as the anti-social porno monster with a Jenna Jameson screen saver and a weekly email updates from AVN.

When I lived in Madagascar people used to shit on the periphery of my yard every few days. I would look up from my desk and see some mischievous 12-year-old or a woman headed back out to the countryside after market day, squatting in the long yellow grass where a curb might have been had the scene been moved to America. If they would catch me staring at them emptying their bowels, they would say hello as if they had just stopped to tie a shoelace or pick up some dropped papers.

Sex was also conducted without much thought to the immediate surroundings. Families of six or eight lived in single-room huts, and when husband and wife or boyfriend and girlfriend wanted to have sex, it necessarily happened with a room full of relatives dozing right next to the lovers. Confronting those most basic physical functions was unavoidable, and it became meaningless.

Living in an apartment building in a big city should, theoretically, be similar. When I lie down to sleep at night, my head is probably four feet away from my older neighbor's head. Two sheets of dry wall and some fuzzy pink insulation is all that separates us. When I snore, I'm sure it reverberates through the walls, when I share my bed with a woman I'm sure the sounds of sex are unavoidable.

When the only sounds I hear from her apartment are the announcer building up drama for the big finale on Dancing with the Stars it makes me sad. Is that how things end up? Thinking of her body, swollen with age, slack and speckled, still writhing on her bed, twisting the sheets, mixing her sweat with someone else's made me smile. I wanted to think of her in that way. I wanted that experience to be something she still sought out.

After a few more minutes of teeth-brushing I realized it wasn't my elder neighbor, but the Guatemalan couple directly above me having sex. The moaning and the dull thud against the mattress sounding like a loop, two people perpetually falling, grappling with each other against the rush of air and the unavoidable gravity pulling on their naked bodies.

Macho Voce, or Women Who Sound Like Men

I once emailed a woman who I thought was very pretty on an internet dating service. She was blonde and wore scarves. In one picture she was dancing in a turquoise dress, twirling towards the camera with a grin, her face flushed and ruddy. She reminded me of Meryl Streep, simultaneously firm and fragile, lovely and unapologetic.

She gave me her number and asked me to call her a few days later. I called her one night as I was leaving work, walking through the empty parking lot in the cold air. When she answered her voice sounded completely different from the impression I had gotten from her pictures. It was husky and insulated, an octave below my own nasally drone. She sounded like a cartoon character; an some exaggerated reduction borrowed from a Saturday Night Live sketch.

I felt a touch of giddiness pressing her number into my phone. I was ready to wash off the lingering touch of office lights and cubicle beige with some flirty wordplay. Hearing her voice made all that hopeful suggestion feel painfully vapid and useless. Her voice was humorless and deliberate, like a Vice-Principal. I felt like we should have been talking about anthropology or bird migration.

I like to imagine women I'm dating with shaved heads to see if I would still find them attractive. It's easy to create an insinuated image of who you want to be with fashion and body decoration, but absent all those outward vanities is there still an attraction? I am vain. I stare at myself in the mirror daily. When I go to the bathroom at work, I almost always spend an extra thirty seconds looking into my own eyes in the mirror. I am still surprised by how many particular details there are in my own appearance that I have almost no connection with.

The body is always the first thing I'm attracted to, usually the face. I recall conversations with women I've been attracted to, spending minutes barely listening, stealing the details of their bodies. The soft wrinkles of the lips, a freckled eyelid, the bony ridges of the sternum, the bawdy smell of their breath caught in between perfume and lip gloss. I've seen that same look returned to me, running my mouth off about some impassioned idea while a woman stares at my glasses or jawline, trying to listen while twisting her hair or fiddling with a shirt.

It feels like I'm with a stranger in moments like these. I can feel my body like some opaque box covering up the truer parts inside. It's like waking up in the morning with my arm twisted unnaturally under my neck. The circulation is cut off and the limb is dead weight, immobile, dangling from the rest of my body like a helpless anchor. When there's nothing else to hold onto, the body is the easiest thing to reach for, to convince yourself that there's a reason to hang on to someone.

I still liked the woman once I got over the shock of hearing her voice. We spoke for a few minutes, then agreed to talk later in the week to setup something for the weekend. She called me a few days later and left a voicemail. I called her back and left her a voicemail, and I never heard from her again. Maybe it was the tinny sound of my voice.

Making Love to ESPN

I used to play high school football. I was obsessed with the NFL when I was younger and there were a few years in my life where I thought my destiny lay in professional sports. Sundays were an exhausting waste during football season. I would wake up early and inhale pre-game prognostication, watch random early games with teams I didn't care about, and make mental notes about random position players for use in comparative analysis. Who's the best right guard in the AFC? Does the 46 defense have a place in the league anymore? With the sun going down and eight hours heedlessly tossed away, I would turn the TV off and realize the weekend was suddenly over, I had done nothing, and my favorite team had lost an away game with a fourth quarter defensive lapse. When I was 10 I actually cried one Monday night when the Raiders lost to the Jets in a game that effectively knocked them out of playoff contention.

There are a lot of women who profess a shared love of sports. They claim to get along better with men than with other women, prefer beer to wine, like watching ESPN and wearing a big foam Number One hand on gameday. You see them every now and then, at sports bars or Super Bowl parties, wearing team jerseys and talking third-down percentages with the barrel-gutted dudes waging a group assault on a pitcher of hefeweizen. It's like being in a strip club and watching a woman with self-possessed swagger move up to the stage with a fistful of dollar bills. It's not that it's so strange to imagine a woman being interested in sports, but I don't understand the impulse for a woman to try and identify with the underlying culture of sports, the sloth, the statistical road to nowhere, the pornographic explosion of team logos and colors, the desperate clinging to the loose storyline of the season every Sunday night, trying to postpone the postgame sobriety as long as possible.

I spent a winter in Prague in my early 20s. I rented an attic room in a hostel in the suburbs for $225 a month, and spent most of my mornings and afternoons clattering away on an old typewriter I had packed into my duffel bag. On Sunday nights I would walk downtown and find an internet café to check in with the NFL. There weren't any places to stream games live so I would sit and stare at a small pop-up window with a list of statistics and a written description of every play. Kaufman carries for two yard gain. 2nd down and 8.

It wasn't quite an addiction, but it was a lonely attempt to connect to a community. The language of sports, the biblical arcana of the NFL rulebook, the secret conclusions carried in random statistics, the crotch shaking energy of cheering in unison with 60,000 other people; it's all a way of gaining an identity without having to risk anything.

Shortly after that winter I stopped caring about professional sports. I lost track of who the new SportsCenter anchors were, I missed out on the Cinderella stories of yesterday's worst teams turning into playoff contenders, I missed all the controversies about inappropriate celebration dances, spats between teammates, superstars unhappy with their coaches, the salary hold-outs, the retirements, the steroid scandals, and the fallout of someone trying to board a plane with some cocaine in their carry-on bag. The story in professional sports is always the same.

Following an NFL season is like reading the same book year after year after year. There are variations – nuances and subtle shifts in meaning float to the surface – but the larger story is identical. Someone always wins, someone always loses. The winners work better together than the losers, they understand their weaknesses better, compensate for them, stick to the game plan, get some lucky breaks, and win. Last year it was New York, this year it's Tennessee, next year it'll be Jacksonville. The names and faces will be different. The jargon will be the same.

Sports is such a permanent ballast for so many relationships.

I wish there were statistics for the prevalence of sex on Sunday nights during football season. How many men get plastered watching other men brutalize one another, come home buzzed and filled with the sense memory of cheerleaders and take to their wives or girlfriends with elephantine urgency? How many women have to compete with Sports Center on Sunday nights for attention and a little empathy?

Maybe it's a welcome respite. The subconscious knowledge that you can count on some time every week where you don't have to worry about your partner, where you can part ways for a little while and be your own separate selves; maybe it's a relief. Coming back together after a day alone could refresh the appreciation you each have for one another.

But how appreciative could someone be for a man stumbling home with the rancid breath of hot wings and Miller Lite, in the male equivalent of a muumuu? How many men piston themselves into a lather on top of their women, get up for another beer, and then wind up in their sweaty underwear on the couch hypnotized by the 11PM Sports Center? Who'll make that porno? I would watch it.

Having Sex at Weddings Redux

I was a bridesmaid in my friend S's wedding in Philadelphia one year. I flew in on a Thursday night and checked into a hotel down the street from Rittenhouse Square. I was a wreck. It was two weeks after N left for New York and I was still reeling in sadness. I did not have my bridesmaid face on. S had asked me to give a speech at the reception. I wrote out a disjointed raft of words on the flight over, crying quietly above my laptop hoping the random stranger sitting next to me wouldn't notice. S#2 was going to be at the wedding too. I met her in person once on a trip to visit S once before but nothing came of it. When I landed in Philly S#2 was already there and we met for a drink.

We went to a dingy bar that allowed smoking and served twenty-five cent hot dogs. The first time I had met S#2 I was clutched with anxiety. Everyone in the group kept nudging me into hitting on her. Anything less than sex in a bar bathroom would have been a disappointment for them. I rebelled against the pressure by ignoring S#2 for most of the night, and when I did speak to her it was about impenetrable topics like the score in Midnight Cowboy and the difference between ketchup and catsup.

S#2 and I were among the first of the long-distance wedding party to arrive in Philly. At the bar she ordered Maker's Mark and Budweiser as if it were a single drink. I went round for round with her, smoking (indoors!) and eating hot dogs. By the time the fourth round arrived I wasn't sure I should be drinking whiskey anymore. My tongue felt heavy in my mouth and I could feel the muscles in my neck going slack. I had been drunk under the table. S and her fiancée met us as I started asking the waitress for water, hoping S#2 wouldn't notice that I was now ignoring the full glass of whiskey in front of me and taking sheepishly small sips of beer.

After closing down the bar we walked back to our hotel, picking up some pizza along the way. It was late May. The city was hot and muggy at 2AM. I had just pierced my nipple and felt a craven urge to take my shirt off while we walked. And so I did. A garbage truck drove by and honked at me as I tottered along the street gutter. It felt good to be drunk. I was cheating, I knew, but it was still nice to actually feel good for a while; to not be swept away on the kaleidoscopic dirge of little memories of N that would otherwise have been spinning around my imagination. Glimpses of her bare feet on my hardwood floor. The taste of her mouth in the morning when I would nudge it open for a first kiss. The angle of her eyes, looking distractedly out the window. The tenuous shake in her voice at karaoke, nervous in a near deserted Chinatown dive bar. I had been living in a silent flood and it felt nice to be numb to it for a few hours.

S#2 and I went back to my hotel room, which I was sharing with my friend B. We ate pizza and watched cable. B announced that she was going to bed and went to the bathroom to brush her teeth. S#2 looked at me and started describing some video she had seen on YouTube, trying to convince me of how funny it was. I was skeptical. She asked me to come up to her room to watch the video on her laptop. There are only so many times in a man's life that a woman asks him back to her room at 3AM to watch YouTube. Here was my moment, suddenly. That mythic window of experience had opened up before me, halfway between amateur porn and a freshman pickup line. I accepted.

We got to her room, a narrow closet with a twin bed. I sat on the bed and she fetched her laptop from the desk then sat beside me on the bed. I started kissing her while she opened the web browser. She kept typing with one eye on the screen while we kissed. The video played. It was less charming than advertised. I made fun of her for thinking it was funny. She protested, defending her taste and sense of humor. We started kissing again. After a while we were in our underpants. I felt overwhelmed by

her body. It was so new and different. I felt the twinge of kaleidoscopic sadness again. I closed my eyes and cupped her face
between my hands and kissed her. It was jarring to open them
again and see her, a shock of blond hair, blue eyes, and pale beige
freckles. This was not N.

We kissed for another hour, trying to jack each other off. I
didn't have condoms, and I didn't care whether or not she did. It
was close to sunrise. My drunkenness was evaporating into a
tired, pulsing distraction. As the numbness wore away I could
feel sadness welling up inside my chest, like a ball of dim light,
a sunrise over some polluted winter city. I looked at the clock
and told her I should probably get to sleep. The wedding
rehearsal was in the morning, and there was a lot of work to do.

I got dressed and went back to my room. The next night the
entire wedding party went out after the rehearsal dinner. S#2 and
I arrived separately. We looked at each other across the bar, intermittently. I felt sheepish and conflicted. I was sober again and
didn't want to hook up anymore that weekend. My head was
scrambled and my heart was upside down. But I liked her. There
are few things I like less than telling people 'no.' I didn't even
know if she had any lingering interest in me. We avoided each
other all night, then as I was leaving with the group I had come
with I walked over to her. We made small talk, I asked how she
was getting home, treading conversational water, then gave her
a kiss and took off.

The next day I had to give a speech at the reception. I was
terrified. Giving a speech at a wedding is mortifying. Bridging
the gap between joyful pith and meaningful intimacy in front of
a huge group of distracted onlookers is terrifying. Everyone that
went before me was perfect, alternating personal anecdote with
coy jokes about the bride's or groom's personality quirks. After
postponing as long as I could B shoved me up to the podium. My
veins dilated and my hands were sweating on the microphone. I
skimmed the room for half a second, then looked down at my

shiny leather boots. I had written a thousand words on my laptop, ambling sentences riddled with semi-colons and inconclusive parentheticals. I tried to pull the form of it from memory.

My point, like most things I try to express, was over complicated and awkwardly phrased. Words hung off the main idea like an oversized suit on a skinny man. It was all vaguery and guesswork. When you love someone you want their partner to be someone who'll take care of them the way you'd take care of them if you could. S still teases me over the speech. Everyone was really funny and short and then I went up there and made a sappy puddle of myself in public for a few minutes. 'What the hell was that?' she asked me a few weeks later.

That night we all stayed out late. I had moved to a different hotel a mile away from the hotel I had stayed at the first night, to be closer to the reception. We closed another bar and I wound up alone again with S#2. I walked her back to her hotel. I stopped at the steps to the front door. She stood a few steps up and lingered, both of us holding on to small talk. I yawned and said I was exhausted. I moved in and gave her a hug and kiss on the cheek. I backed away down the street and she walked up the remaining steps and disappeared into the hotel.

I drunk dialed N on my way home, talking into the empty vacuum of her voicemail as I stumbled through the old streets of downtown Philly. The red and brown bricks melded together into a dull crimson under the street lights. The only thing I had left were words, and I sent them through the phone mic in a soft voice, meandering through all the details of where I was, what I had been doing, and what time of morning it was. It felt nice for a few seconds, almost like touching, the 1s and 0s being translated into sound waves, recorded in some master server, archived for 14 days, played back later, on a Sunday morning, looking out a window at the bright and sunny sidewalk. It felt like I was somewhere else entirely.

Then I hung up, drunk and alone in Philadelphia.

Old Love Letters, or Things That Got Thrown Away in the Move

Moving is stupid. I had two months to get everything organized for my move to New York and I still wound up the night before with my four bags stuffed to bursting. After all the planning there remained a pile of scattered detritus, all the random crap that I wanted to take but couldn't find space for. I felt like a caveman staring at two sticks and kindling, trying to figure out if there was any other way beyond the obvious to accomplish what I wanted.

One of the things I've carried with me through every move since I left home is a plastic filling container that my mom gave me when I was 16. I used it to store old letters, birthday cards, and scraps of writing amassed since my adjective-laden teenage years (one of these days I'll address that habit for real).

I looked at the rectangular box filled with old memories that I hadn't looked at in years. I knew it had to go.

I unfastened the flimsy metal clasp and dumped all the scattered papers out onto the floor. 'Only the most important stuff is coming along,' I thought.

A big proportion of all the old scraps were drugstore cards for graduation, birthdays, Christmas, past moves. Cards I had received in the late nineties were oversized and ostentatious. They unfolded like small erector sets with paper scaffolding and puffy text written in sparkles. Inside these salutary behemoths were paper leaflets that unfolded like tablecloths. There was enough room to write a chapter in a novel, but most had a paragraph or less of handwritten text. 'We love you!' 'We're proud!' 'Hope you have a great day!' 'Congratulations!'

I threw most of them out.

Then I had the uncomfortable surprise of finding some old love letters to J, which I never sent. I became friends with her my senior year in high school. My old English teacher told me she had a crush on me one day, and so I made an effort to talk to her. I was all elbows and awkwardness, which is why I think we never got past being friends. But I wanted to. We would wander through the newly-opened Barnes & Noble together. We'd sit at Krakatoa Café in the late afternoons, drinking black coffee and arguing about books.

We started emailing when we were in college, but she grew distant. She joined a sorority and became entrenched in her theater program. We were both surrounded by tens of thousands of new people and possibilities. The incentive to stay in touch dimmed.

Before I let go, I had one last flush of emotion. I was working at Yosemite for the summer between my first and second year of college. I felt like I was in an alien world most days, far away from the safely structured decadence of my college life. Not everyone was a middle-class kid on their way to a lucrative career sprung from a paid-for education.

I would quote from the letter, but thankfully I'm writing this on a plane and it's tucked away in my checked luggage in the cargo hold below. Re-reading that letter to her, written in a 19-year-old's emotional upheaval one desperate summer was mortifying. It was like looking at a terrible picture of yourself, with the lights and angles all wrong, so that you look like someone else entirely.

There can't have been any period of time when I was so needy and sniveling, so uncertain. So willing to make someone else an answer to all those adolescent wants, like a nostalgic voodoo doll for happiness.

It was three pages, front and back, on spiral-bound notebook paper. The last paragraph trailed off into an incomprehensible attempt to define what I wanted from her. It ended mid-sentence.

At least I didn't send it. It's hard to remember, it's so long ago now. But I must have reread what I had written and realized there was no way to send that to another person. I was a driveling teenage mess, and the fact that I was writing a rhetorical pitch for why we should make a go at romance together was a sure sign that our friendship had run its course. I wasn't talking to her anymore, I was writing to myself, spewing my own uncertain issues at the paper and planning to send them to her expecting a solution.

I never sent it. But I brought that letter with me. It's gone from Yosemite, Fresno, Los Angeles, China, Madagascar, San Francisco, and now it's own it's way to New York, 12 years later. The dried up tissue paper from one summer when I was a wet teenage mess.

J, you were a lousy friend. And I was worse.

Super Macho Man Slumber Party

A few months before I moved to New York my friend P came to visit for a few days. He arrived on a weeknight and we went out for dinner and then had drinks at a bar with some other friends. We got home close to 2AM and spent another half hour talking in the darkness of my studio apartment, him asleep on the guest mattress at the foot of my bed. I felt a little distracted by the specter of getting up early for work the next day, but it was nice to finally talk to another man without the jocular strictures that seem to guide normal mantalk.

I've known P for years. We went to high school together, but we actively disliked one another during those years. We ran into each other again our junior year in college and had an awkward catch-up conversation out of obligation, exchanged numbers, and made a vague date to hang out. P called a few days later and we wound up going out with my roommates and.surprisingly, had a good time together. We both have stone dry senses of irony and a sardonic view on socializing.

In the interim P has become as close a friend as I have. There isn't anything about me I haven't told him. He's seen me at my lowest and highest. We complement each other well. P is more socially adept than I am, and I find it much easier to be my truer, unfiltered self when he's in the room to buffer the immature acid undertone. P also has a tendency to be self-serious and I think my immaturity brings out his ebullient side.

P's fantastically successful and a good ballast to my impulsive idealism. Life is hard at every step of the way. There are no easy years. Deciding to move to New York was terrifying. It was nice to talk with P about that and about N in the dark, without any distractions or need for posturing.

People tend to want answers, direct conclusions that they can walk away from. People want there to be a reason for things to be the way they are. There has to be some invisible algebra guiding our collective subconscious and seeing an experience written about without concretizing terms is cause for troubleshooting. If your date went like that, it must be because of this. This is especially true for men. We're not encouraged to be honest with one another.

Men maintain, we compete, and we reassure each other that everything is fine. The idea of two grown men lying in darkness, speaking to each other in intimate terms is alarmingly vulnerable. I get a lot of guff from many of my more manly friends for the way I sometimes write, the endless self-analysis and the indemnifying confessions of imperfect form and thought. I write like a puff. It's disgusting. Men aren't supposed to be weak and uncertain of where the next step lies, they're supposed to be cheerful oafs, easily satisfied with beer, pussy, and the white noise of a scoreboard.

Men hold hands with each other in China. The tendency of same sex friends to be physically affectionate isn't unique to China, but it's the first place I encountered it. I was surprised and uncomfortable the first time one of my male students grabbed my hand as we were walking to a row of street vendors on campus for lunch. My hands sweat terribly. They used to drip small puddles in high school and I developed a huge complex about it. My stomach would drop when someone held their hand out for me to shake, and the thought of holding a woman's hand was nauseating. It would have pointed to an irrefutably physical proof of my imperfection, my weakness.

I don't think I've never told P I loved him. I do, but those aren't terms we use. What good is it telling another man you love him? I've told him everything else.

Breaking Up Is Hard To Do,
or Leaving Home

My least favorite thing about the holidays is the leaving. I enjoy the family rivalries, the inevitable clashes of different threads of family and friends. I'm indifferent to the added stresses of holiday crowds in airports and on the freeways, but saying goodbye over and over again is hard. We can live farther away from the people we love and stay in touch with the various digital wonderments of fiber-optics and satellites orbiting overhead, but there is no replacement for sharing the same space. That's the inevitable conclusion I arrive at every year during the holidays. Arriving home, dropping the ungainly weight of my bags, opening the windows to freshen the stifled air of my dormant apartment, looking out on the streets below, familiar but filled with strangers flowing past in their indifferent rushes, I feel small and alone.

I take my parents for granted. As they age and I sink further into my own separate self they seem like weathered fragments from my past. I remember a time when they were the alpha and the omega of my life, the twin horizons over which the sun rose and set every day. I remember sitting on my father's lap reading The Little Mermaid aloud in the library at University of Texas, Austin, where he spent a summer teaching when I was four. He was a titan, his voice shook through my body as it animated each line of the fairytale. It was a force of nature, like a rainstorm of smiling words and warm imagination.

I remember the indulgent swoon of being in love with my mother. I crawled into bed with her and my dad one Sunday when I was three, hanging from her neck kissing her cheeks and lips. When she would take me shopping with her before I had started school I would venture out into the department store sprawl and bring back tight mini-skirts and red nail polish for her. I wanted her to show herself as the diaphanous monument she was to me.

All those experiences are tricks of perspective. Age and inexperience help to curve the lens in a way that makes the world seem intimate and hyper-real, but it changes again and again. That doesn't make those experiences any less real. I hate leaving my parents home after the holidays every year. I inevitably grow bored and stir crazy there, eating their food, listening to them argue, watching their cable, and making nice with their friends. Leaving always feels terrible. I spend my last hours in their home quietly packing, sulking and feeling leery about wherever it is that I'm off to next. It's like breaking up with the same person over and over again, but each break-up is framed by the incremental creep of age.

I don't understand break-ups where people walk away from one another and never look back. Relationships are hard work, and the idea of lifelong coupling is a statistical Hail Mary. But saying 'I love you' is a concession of permanence for me. It doesn't mean you agree to have fun together until things get too painful and then you agree to call things off and never talk to one another again. Those onset hardships are inevitable, as is the reframing of one's point of view over time. But how can you stop loving someone?

I've always experienced breaking up is a concession to semantics. You reach a point where it stops making sense to keep your own path hemmed in by your partner's; it stops being what you want. I've never fallen out of love. My parents were the first two people I ever fell in love with. I don't want to live with them anymore, nor am I interested in having them directly involved in guiding my vessel as I keep pressing forward into new places. But I don't want to let them go. I loved them, and I love them still, even if they don't much resemble the romantic titans of my infancy.

Their faces have changed improbably over the years, without

my noticing. Their physical infirmities are full of new wrinkles, unassuming new pill bottles in the medicine cabinets. They make strange noises when they breathe. My childhood toys are all gone. I sleep on the guest room now. The room I grew up in is hundreds of miles away from my parent's new house. So it's sad when I pack my bags and walk to the front door, headed to the airport, knowing that there's no forgotten scrap left behind in the guestroom. The semantic ties have evaporated. Love is like gravity. I know I'll be back next year, and the year after that, but only for a little while, so long as they're there.

Moving to New York

After seven months of planning, saving, angling, 13 boxes, and 170 pounds of luggage, I finally moved to New York.

Moving is the best and worst of everything in life. There's nothing more exciting than starting again; going to a new place and fighting to figure out how you will fit into it. And there are few things as dispiriting as seeing everything you own reduced to a pile of banker's boxes and black duffel bags. All the excitement and anticipation is framed in a fearful vertigo.

I've made a lot of major moves in my life and I remember the night before each, staring at the final collection of luggage. That's it, that's all I have. This is my only remaining physical footprint, and I have to strap it to my back now and heft it to the airport and fling it into the unknown.

I stayed up all night both times before I left for Peace Corps. The first night I stayed up packing and repacking. When I left for Madagascar I spend the night at a friend's Halloween party and then drove back to my parents house at 4AM. I had a 9AM flight and I decided to make some coffee and stay up the last few hours playing a game called Super Mario Sunshine.

The night before I left for New York, I stayed up till close to midnight wrestling my bags. Then I gave up and went to sleep. My mattress had been recycled so I slept on a yoga mat in my friend's apartment in Berkeley. I had strange dreams all night. In one I was in a symphony hall that turned into a dormitory. My ex-girfriend from China was there and I wandered around trying to find a free bunk to sleep in.

In another dream I was having sex with someone I'd never seen before, standing up with her leg propped across my waist. I kept waking up every hour, checking my cell phone to see what time it was, paranoid I would oversleep. I got up at 5:15AM, minutes before I had set the alarm to go off.

I felt awkward on the train, my four big pieces of luggage sticking out amidst the early-morning commuters. I felt numb and wished I had caffeine. I kept imaging the cheap duffel bag I bought for $8.99 in the Mission ripping open along its bulging seams, spilling all my belongings into the aisle.

The worst part of moving is the uncertainty, like a photograph of someone throwing a bucketful of water into the air, the particulate globs suspended in motion above the ground.

All those feelings are useless, bouncing around in an entropic vacuum with nothing but speculation to keep them in check. They all feel so immediate and crucial in those hours in flux, suspended between two points on a map, strung out on a piece of yarn connecting them. As soon as you land, they become absurd, disconnected from the daily realities of wherever you wind up.

And then I landed in New York. To begin. And begin again.

Long Distance Lovers

I was having lunch with my friend M one day and she mentioned a girlfriend who'd been writing back and forth with a man through a dating service for an extended period of time. He lived in a different country and they'd never met in person.

It's easy to imagine this is the worst face of internet dating: two people so lonely for companionship that they're willing to spend big chunks of their time emailing their daily devotional thoughts and fears. It might be one thing to have an intimate correspondence with an old friend who lives far away, but the idea of doing it with a stranger has an undercurrent of desperation.

When I was 22 I wound up emailing a woman who had gone to my high school. A mutual friend thought that we might have something in common. We were both writers, read too much, and had a similar taste for deviance and disruption. She still lived in Fresno and I had been in Los Angeles for more than four years. I didn't know anyone there anymore, and the idea that I might still have a friend in the town where I grew up, a writer no less, made me happy.

We started emailing and got along as predicted. We picked up each other's musical references and had patience for arcane arguments about DH Lawrence versus Anais Nin. In hindsight, it was an embarrassing scrum of mutual assurance that we were separate and better than all those other slackjaws; a short-term emotional cocoon for the overly sensitive post-graduate.

Our emails gave way to phone calls, and after a few months I decided it was time to stop ebbing around the edges. I asked her if I could come up and visit her one weekend. She said yes.

I had no idea what she looked like. The only point of reference I had was a hazy photo from my high school yearbook. She was pale and freckly and her lips were small but puffy pink.

I had the mental pre-tingle of sex the whole drive up. It was exciting imagining what she would be like in person. I had come to know her personality well enough, but there was a whole other being there, still unmet. Her body, her mannerisms, rhythms, movements, smells. Her inner self had been a good partner so far. I was hopeful that the physical side would be a good match as well.

When she opened the door to her apartment I was overwhelmed by stale air and cat piss. She was wearing dirty blue sweat pants and a baggy t-shirt with blotchy stains spattered across it. Whatever might have been tingling inside me earlier came to a stop.

Suddenly, the idea of a long weekend with her company seemed like an insurmountable trudge. I had imagined a lithe kink-sprite tumbling from the pages of Delta of Venus. Instead, I was entering the zone with a pallid introvert with an over-tolerance for the stench of her cat's bodily waste. For a moment I imagined turning around, walking back to my car, and driving the four hours back to LA.

'Come in,' she said.

We talked for a little while. I helped her with the last bit of tidying up, which my arrival had so noticeably interrupted. The sun was going down and we decided to get some beer and watch a movie. I was nervous and tried to keep her at arm's length with conversation, hoping I could cover my recoil with some affable chatter about anything so long as it was non-sexual. She remained quiet, answering in barely audible mumbles and short clips that I couldn't reconcile with the woman I had gotten to know over the phone.

After a few beers and an hour of an old movie she became animated. We were sitting side by side on her couch, awash in a sea of cat hair. She reached for a small tin of lip balm and put some on. She asked if she could put some on me.

My body stiffened and I tried to keep my eyes locked on the

television. This was the moment I had been dreading. She was going to try and seduce me now. I had hoped I could passively joke my way through the weekend as if we were just good buddies catching up. But she was ready for sex. I figured out some terrible excuse for not wanting to put on lip balm ('Why? I don't really feel like I need it.') but she persisted. After a few minutes, we came to a compromise. I would put on lip balm but I would apply it myself.

Not deterred, she bent down at my feet and started undoing my shoelaces. I was wearing heavy boots and it took some effort to unlace them. I knew what was happening but I didn't know how to tell her no. I wished there would have been a button to push or a placard I could hold up that could settle things. Instead she pulled off my boot and smelled the inside with a giant inhale, all while looking me in the eye.

'Do you want to kiss me?' she asked.

I told her we should just watch the movie. She threw my boot across the room and then leaned over me, lowering her mouth to mine. I leaned away and held my forearm up to keep us separate. She pulled away and looked at the floor. She sat down next to me on the couch and after a few minutes I heard her crying.

We finished the movie in silence and then went to bed. I lay beside her all night, rigid and afraid to move for fear of brushing against her.

Affinity for someone's personality is not sex. I had no idea.

The Celebrity You Most Resemble

My friend C sometimes teases me with the idea that I look like Nick Nolte. Just hearing his name insinuates a black metallic fear in the bottom of my heart. We have similar facial structures, no cheekbones, pursed lips, brows prone to furrowing. I'd be okay with the analogy if Nick Nolte's index of attractiveness stopped in the late seventies, maybe somewhere around The Deep. That's not the image of Nick Nolte that I have. That may have been who he once was, but it isn't who he's become. The Nick Nolte I know is the one that looks like a scarecrow and passes out on the floor in airports, clutching his folded glasses like some confused professor after a quart of hot toddies. It's a scary comparison because it reminds me that I have no idea who it is that I'll become as the years continue to deflower me.

Over the summer I started to look at people on the sidewalk, in coffee shops, sitting at bars and I would imagine how they would age. It might have been a delusional skill, but I began seeing eager young 20-something's age into liver-spotted 50- and 60-year-olds. I started doing this with old people too. Grumpy old women and tired old men in outmoded shades of gray and brown easily morphed into their lithe younger selves, with tight skin and sparkling eyes.

There aren't many people whom I've gotten to see age over a long period of time. With my parents and myself the process has been so gradual that I've barely noticed any change at all. I find it hard to look in the mirror and see how I'm different from my teenage self. I know I am, but I don't know what it is that's different. I have the same experience when I'm with my parents. My 63-year-old father is indistinguishable from his 35-year-old self. It's jarring to go back and look at old photos and be reminded of just how much he has changed. I forget about the white hair, the new wrinkles, the loosening skin. It's so easy to look past all that in the course of the days and weeks that sneak up on us.

I'm bad at accepting compliments. It makes me uncomfortable, and I've learned to cover up that discomfort with an aloof disinterest. I have no idea how attractive I really am. I don't have any interest in the general criterion of what makes someone attractive or not. It's usually either symmetry or conformity. Clothes can make people more attractive with a subtle suggestion of someone else, emulating the style of some social group, you can subconsciously insinuate yourself into their circle. Or you can just celebrate the fact that your eyes are evenly spaced and your body is proportionate and let the oohs and ahhs fall where they may.

It's always surprising to see someone drawn to me, charmed by whatever energy or image I'm translating into in their minds. I know that I have attractive qualities and am comfortable with the idea of people being drawn to them. But it can also be disembodying to get complimented for something you have no control over, like symmetry. It's always nice to feel desirable, but when the root of that desirability is the result of some genetic gamble, the compliment stops being about who you are. It's like when a stranger sees you from afar and mistakes you for an acquaintance and waves before realizing their mistake.

So when C tells me I look like Nick Nolte, even when she protests and insists that it's the young Nick Nolte that she means, I still panic. Nick Nolte is a paean to the transience of all the things we tend to value in our world. Looks, talent, success, a great mustache. Who would have thought that brawny man with the romantic squint and the wind-swept hair would one day turn into a prune-faced drunk lying on the floor in baggy pajamas? It's even more terrifying to imagine that he must surely feel the same on the inside now as he did when he was young and desirable. I can imagine Nick Nolte staring at himself in the mirror some mornings, just like I do, touching his face and

finding it indistinguishable from the one he saw years earlier.
The Celebrity I Most Resemble: Nick Nolte.

How to Pick Up a Nurse at the HIV Clinic

I was arguing with my friend P about competition one night. He believes the need to compete overshadows everything in our romantic lives. I don't care. I don't want to compete against the field to wind up with someone who's attractive and successful just to show everyone else that I can. Relationships aren't prizes. They're hard work and require sacrifice. Why would anyone want to compete to get into a bind like that? Why would anyone want to enter into a relationship with someone that they had to convince to join them?

A few weeks earlier I went to get an HIV/STD test. The clinic was intended to serve the needs of high-risk gay men. There was only one woman working there. She was short, had curly hair, and walked around with an eager smile and beaming eyes. After listening to her talk to some of the other volunteers I figured out that it was her first day on the job.

An hour later she came out into the lobby with a file in her hand and called my name. As I followed her down the short hallway to the testing room I felt a small thread of nervousness unspooling in my midsection. I was already jumpy about the test, I hadn't expected to be going through it with someone I was attracted to.

She held the door open for me and I sat in a chair against the far wall. She closed the door behind her and sat down with her overflowing smile. For the next 10 minutes we talked about my recent sexual history. Coming clean about all the lewd, kinky, and potentially infectious behavior I'd engaged in is not high on my list of things to do with a women I find attractive.

We talked about what kinds of fluids have been in my mouth, my preference for anal play, and I retold the story of my first STD. You're cute, and also I used to have dick snails.

As I was going over all the unflattering proclivities of my

sexual self, she seemed unfazed. She nodded during particularly embarrassing details with normalizing statements, 'Yeah, that's totally common. I know a lot of people who are into that.' As I rambled, her fingers were in constant motion along the hem of her shirt running along the edge of the fabric and skin. She tilted her head to the side when I tilted mine, she laughed out loud at all my nervous puns.

It came time to draw blood. She rolled her chair next to mine and straddled my knee with her legs. She took the inner part of my forearm in both hands and gently ran her thumb up and down over the crook of my elbow to find a vein. I'm lanky and have veiny forearms. It was a hot morning and I'd walked a mile and a half to get to the clinic. My veins were presenting.

She said she was having trouble finding a vein. She asked me to hold out my other arm. She took it and ran her fingers along the skin of my inner arm, leaving a warm tingly trail in their wake. Neither of us said anything. Five seconds went by. Ten seconds. Our heads were a foot away from each other, my knee was inches from her lap. I could smell the soap on her skin, the soft hint of detergent from her clothes. I had started sweating a little on the walk over. There was probably some musky remnant of it mixing with my Apricot deodorant.

She leaned in closer, looking at the veins coming down my forearm. Her breast drifted across my hand as she moved. It happened again when she sat back.

After the test was over we kept talking, our words trying to prolong the last few minutes we would have together with whatever meager excuses we could find. We talked about travel. She told me about a trip to India, 'with my boyf- someone I was traveling with.' A few minutes later she made the same edit, changing an unformed 'b' word into 'the person I live with.'

I told her I was moving to New York in a week. She mentioned meeting in New York three different times, though she had no plans to come to the city and didn't mention any friends there.

I must have been rambling, my sentences coming out like blushing torrents of self-deprecation. I wanted to ask her out. I knew I wouldn't because I was leaving in a week (and for N!) though my attraction to her was strong, it wasn't unfamiliar. It was sporting and friendly and fun, but it wasn't overwhelming. It was just a surprise to find someone like her in a place like that.

When you really like someone you don't need to compete for anything. You don't need to prove anything, because the simple act of sharing your time and thoughts is entertaining enough. You can convince people to like you with a little thought and social manipulation.

It's like doing a card trick, you can convince people that they're seeing something extraordinary when its just sleight of hand. With the right ones you just have to be honest and find a way to stick together for as long as you can. Staying together is always the harder part. Convincing someone to come home with you is easy. It's a cheap trick and the payoff is a lie.

How you pick up a nurse: go get an STD check.

Lying Lovers, or the Padded Bra

A friend once admitted to a habit of telling men she is about to have sex with that she wears a padded bra. This reminded me of a few horrific moments I spent with an old girlfriend when we had sex for the first time.

I've never dated women with large breasts and I don't really care one way or the other. I've been with a lot of women who had smaller cup sizes and wore padded bras. These bras always struck me as bizarre machinery.

I admire a nice bra, a functional girding, ornamented with lace and Victorian detail. There's something honest about the combined vanity and purpose of a bra. If the weight must be supported, then let it be supported beautifully. Extra padding in the cup doesn't have any purpose other than to mislead. Seeing a padded bra is always faintly disappointing. I never feel duped that someone's naked body didn't live up to the promise of the swells and slopes of the clothed silhouette. The idea that person I'm with wanted me to think they were something else, even superficially, is sad.

After spending an evening together my ex and I moved to her bedroom together. We had kissed on the couch for a long time, slowly and without any great sense of urgency. I slid my hand over her body and she demurred. She would pull back for a moment and smile at me coyly, and then we would kiss again. I thought she wanted to move slowly and so I didn't try and escalate things.

After a while, I was on top of her and began undoing her bra. I wanted to feel her skin against my own. The bra was a jarring obstruction every time it rubbed against my chest. We kept kissing as I slid the bra down and moved my hand across her bare breasts for the first time. I immediately panicked.

There was no breast there. Where I thought I might have felt some small mound I found only skin and rib cage. In the darkness it felt almost concave. An idea started to form in my head, her reluctance to escalate things in the living room, the slowness of our kissing, absence of anything beneath her bra. She must have had a mastectomy, I thought. I couldn't come up with any other explanation, so dramatic was the disparity between the poofy B-cup bra and the planar landscape of her upper body.

Am I ready to have sex with a cancer survivor? Is there a proper method for making love to someone who's had a mastectomy? Was I doing something earlier that made her not want to tell me? What does it look like with the light on?

My mind was running away with itself, inventing an elaborate set of irrational conclusions in a few seconds. I was on the verge of asking her about it when she shifted her weight and I felt the thin layer of her breast ripple. I suddenly felt like an ass. She hadn't had a breast removed, it was just that her breasts were exceptionally small and all but disappeared when she was on her back.

I had no issue with her breast size. I wouldn't have given it a second thought had I known to expect it. I wasn't reeling at her body, it was the disparity of the projection and the reality. I wasn't there, naked and in bed with her, because of her body. I wanted to be with her. I didn't want ideals. I wanted particulars, her particulars.

That can be the hardest thing to have faith in when you're having sex with someone for the first time. It's so much easier to let the person see what they want to see, to willfully mislead their gaze to an idyllic exaggeration. It's frightening to not apologize for yourself, to put it out there in all its adorned honesty and trust that whoever it is that you end up with will be able to take it and love it for what it is: a part of you.

Look Ugly in a Photograph

I've never made a New Year's resolution. I have plenty of stupid habits formed during years of slovenly bachelorism. If I were more conscientious I might have taken the opportunity to really commit myself to better posture in 2009, or maybe come to grips with the habit of picking my nose when nobody's looking. As the giddy fizz of one New Year started to recede, there was one thing that started to gnaw at me. I think I take terrible pictures.

I cannot smile in pictures. Most pictures I see of myself vary between an expressionless glare and a hyper-exaggerated clown face. I first realized this taking my senior portrait for the high school yearbook. The photographer prodded me, tried to trick me into laughing with some scat humor, and even goaded me with a stuffed animal, but the best expression I could give him as a closed-mouth grin.

One woman I used to date liked the fact that she couldn't read my expressions, that everything I said came out in the same warbling monotone, words stumbling over each other like strangers trying to avoid close contact in a crowded subway station. Looking at myself in other people's pictures makes me uncomfortable.

There is the superficial vanity, the dread that the package you've come in looks like a dented can of peaches in the discount bin at the grocery store. Someone once compared me to David Koresh after having seen a photo of me. I liked the particular photo because I was smiling, and though it was only half-serious, it's there.

The biggest disappointment I have in seeing pictures of myself isn't the ugliness or unflattering angles, it's the disparity between what I remember of the moment and what remains in two-dimensions days and weeks after the fact. Smiling for the camera is an admitted fakery. No one can improvise genuine happiness on the spot and sustain it for four or five seconds while staring into a machine's lens. The idea that I'm being recorded for posterity makes me freak out. I feel like I'm trapped in a death rictus when I try and hold a smile. My favorite pictures of people I care about aren't the smiling ones, they're the ones with the least amount of artifice in between, showing the undecorated face, the eyes deliberate and open.

If I could give that face in photographs every time I would. But I want to perform. So I squirm and try to leave something interesting for posterity. And it ends up looking like just what it is, a worm squirming.

My New Year's Resolution: be genuine in photographs.

Using Your Words

I usually begin all of my emails with 'heyo.' I'm not sure how I got into this habit. That word isn't a part of my spoken vernacular at all, and I can't think of anyone I know who used it with me first. It's entirely opaque. It sounds arcane, like something an uncle would say in some dusty reference to Archie comics. It's breezy and has some suggested energy behind it, like the thoughtless greeting that a friend would give you while preoccupied with the lingering tentacles of some past task. It's also deeply affectionate. With some people I use the word like a casual brushback to show indifference, but with others, it's a little caress, a gentle thumb stroke across the chin.

The trouble is that all these distinctions happen on my side. They have nothing to do with how my words are received by whomever it is I send them out to. I used to have a penchant for saying the word 'pap.' It's perfectly vulgar, dismissive, and clinical. My friend C has latched onto this word as the singular identifier of a basic revulsion she gets when talking to me some nights. The way I slip it into a conversation about movies or the proper way to batter fried chicken makes her recoil in disgust. 'I can feel my vagina crawling up inside my body when you say that,' she told me the other night after a thoughtless use of the word.

'Pap' has become shorthand for the nature of our friendship; simultaneously intimate and physically repulsive. She lets me tease her with the word, knowing all of its nauseating associations. It's a concession to the final absence of sex between us. Her revulsion would hurt me if I had any sexual interest in her. I'm sure she would be deeply alarmed by how callous and clinical I can sometimes be if we had a physical relationship.

When I use the word with other people it goes unnoticed. It's almost meaningless, falling between the conversational cracks.

It's disappointing that no one else seems to get the same meaning from the word that C immediately plucks out.

When I forced myself back into the dating pen after N left some of the dates I noticed a similar disappointment. I wound up saying the same things over and over again, telling the same stories in the same terms. Going on a string of first dates on exacerbates this. How many times have I told the story of why I moved to San Francisco from LA? How many inquisitive stares have looked at me while I explain how one can earn money writing, and about videogames of all subjects. The words bubble out and evaporate immediately. They have no owner.

Being in a relationship is like sharing a secret language. The same words that people use to buy carrots and talk to their relatives are imbued with eros and intimacy. They become fingers that you can touch someone with, tickling them, pinching them, caressing them. With strangers, they're cold, clinical probes, little pebbles you take turns tossing into each other's metaphysical pond, hoping one will catch somewhere and skip along the surface leaving a rippling trail in its wake.

I still find myself out with other women, realizing that I'm using N's words. I do not think I will ever forget them, nor their secret meaning. I don't like saying that. I want to be glib and pulled together about it. Moving on. Moving forward, ever upward. Then I reach the point in the night where I realize I'm sending all those verbal gestures and little touches to someone who isn't there.

Which is usually when I lean in to kiss my date. Onward, upward.

Tool Academy

Nobody gets anywhere by going home and watching television every night. But that's what happens in a lot of relationships that make it through the swooning haze of early romance. It can be hard to keep improvising activities and romantic goose chases through night corridors of a city. After a few months, the urgency of staying out past midnight every night transforms into a familiar comfort that makes staying in and watching television seem just as inviting. I was reminded of this while watching the first episode of Tool Academy tonight.

I can't watch scripted television shows anymore. I've become a reality show addict, and nothing caters to an addictive personality quite like reality shows. I've spent many Sundays sitting on the couch watching entire seasons of The Real World, Big Brother, Beauty & The Geek, Shot at Love with Tia Tequila, I Love New York, and Celebrity Rehab from start to finish. I've gorged on so much vapid nothingness, quick-cut into mouthwatering bites of outbursts, conflict, and sexual voyeurism; it's a hard comedown to settle in for the night with some plodding episode of crime solving.

I've never dated anyone who shared my affection for reality shows. There's an indignance many people have about it, as if they're better than consuming such exploitive cultural filth. I made N watch something called That's Amore one night when we were still in San Francisco. The show was about a short Italian man who wore three different shirts at a time and had a love consiglieri in the form of a large Alabaman man living in a trailer in the backyard of his mansion. She was not impressed, though she tolerated an episode for my sake.

Reality shows are designed around suggested visual punchlines intended to ridicule their actors in some way. A deadpan cut after a muscle-headed guy with mousse in his hair says something stupid tells the audience what conclusion they're supposed to reach in a split second.

I also like the jealousy reality shows inspires in me. Watching Tool Academy, a show where macho alpha men are sent to reform school to save their failing relationships, I couldn't help curling my toes in envy when all the men pulled off their shirts and stepped into Speedos, flexing their muscled bodies for the camera. The suggestion of physical superiority gooses my ego. It never goes very deep, but it feels good to be taunted a little bit, it's a kind of emotional exercise, like a cat flexing its claws subconsciously in sleep.

Confessing that I like reality television is as embarrassing as the first time you fart around someone new. Both are ubiquitous and both serve a crude function that, despite protestations, everyone has to fulfill sooner or later. It's both intimate and incriminating, an admission or imperfection.

Which is why it kind of felt like smelling my own farts when I was home alone one night and watching the first episode of Tool Academy. I missed not feeling embarrassed about it, framed by N's watching face beside me.

Sleeping Naked

When I was younger I struggled to fall asleep when sharing the bed with a woman. Being so close to another body, hearing their breath, smelling their skin, feeling their inhales nudge their soft bellies against mine; it was sensory overload. I spent nights and nights lying besides women, wide awake. As I got older the foreignness of another body in bed next to me subsided. The persistent touch of the blunter parts of our bodies, the breath, the warm echo of old sex, it all became a comfort instead of a lingering alien encounter.

I've gotten into the habit of walking around my apartment naked in the mornings and on weekends. Being naked in the daytime feels natural. It feels apt, like a precursor to something active, undoubtedly sexual. There's so much to distract in the daytime, the sounds from the street, the intensity of all the details the sunlight brings out, the subconscious urge to go out and be productive. Being naked and alone at night is scary to me. I like the idea that my nudity at night is tied to sex. Being naked with the night sky above, in an empty box stacked on top of dozens of other empty boxes, the loneliness is amplified.

The touch of the cold air and the rustled sheet aren't unsettling because of the nakedness, but because of their indifference to it. Shouldn't a thing that touches me so intimately have more of a purpose? Shouldn't there be more to say with all the waiting nerve endings of my body than to lay limply across it in the dark?

I realized that I hadn't slept naked in months after N left. I tried to sleep naked by myself one night, but it was unsettling. I kept pulling against the sheets, trying to turn away. It was too much sensation to feel the sheets' cotton weave muzzle against my bare skin. And so finally I got up and put on a t-shirt and pajama bottoms. It was cold, I could feel my toes slowly drifting toward numbness on the hardwood floors. The air felt sharp and metallic against my bare arms. I pulled the t-shirt over my head and looked at myself in the closet mirror, happy to think that my pajamas matched, happy that they'd be a gentle buffer against my cruel sheets that only reminded me of all the indifferent spaces between the threads.

Becoming a Virgin Again

My friend S once confessed that he had become a virgin again. This is a phenomenon that occurs when somebody goes for a year or longer without having sex.

I was alarmed to find out that there's actually a name for this kind of thing because it had been almost a year for me too. I've gone on long sojourns without sex in the past, but I'd never stopped to add up the days and weeks and months. I didn't realize there were specific words to categorize people according to lengths of time they'd been without a little wettening of their pants parts.

I am stingy with my sex. One-night stands are fine in theory, but I am not wired to enjoy them soberly. Sex is too intimate and, when my faculties aren't numbed by some substance, being that close to a stranger's body sends my brain into a gyroscopic spasm of disembodiment.

I also avoid anything resembling a relationship whenever I can. It's a combination of selfishness and self-defense. I don't have brakes in relationships. I freefall for people. Knowing that, in combination with the memories of my parents' acrimonious relationship, I have developed an instinctual avoidance of intimacy. And to complete the Freudian circle of hypocrisy, I steer subconsciously towards those things I fear most. So I am an emo-gazing fop who avoids having to live up to the hermetically sealed virtues of my own rhetoric.

I give good advice, but I create all these fragile emotional constructs in my own life and each one inevitably comes crashing down in a tinkling cacophony of shattering china.

I'm comfortable going through extended periods without sex, then. Sex is not a body function for me. It's not a glass of water. It's not a sport. It's not a stress reliever. It's language and intimacy, and thinking that way means there's always less sex on my horizon when I go out for a night.

But for S, the idea that he hadn't had sex in a year was torture. He huffed and puffed, he groaned and strained and cussed. He let loose a dozen variations on the time honored 'I gotta get laid.'

In both China and Madagascar, I heard many graven-faced men tell me that they had to have sex or else they would get sick. Keeping all that sperm trapped inside a man's guts inevitably led to poor health and a shambolic state of mind. It sounded like voodoo logic at the time, but watching S I started to wonder if his sperm hadn't pickled in his brain. He seemed depraved and come-drunk.

What I don't understand about people who need to have sex but don't are their reasons for not having sex. It's not difficult to have sex. You might have to lower your physical standards a bit, or endure some embarrassing bouts of rejection at a bar before finding that special someone to spread her legs; but sex is always attainable. If all a person wants is the sport, the relief, the satisfaction of physical contact, then go get it. It's out there. It's right around the corner. It's probably at some bar five or ten minutes from where you're sitting and reading this.

I remember when S finally had sex again, 13 months after his last encounter. He went out on a first date with a woman, got really drunk, brought her back to his apartment, and had sex with her. I was excited for him when he told me. I was sure this would have been the pivot point where would go from defeated to victorious and confident. He could walk into every room with the pride of a man who had the metaphysical scent of sex hovering in his pants.

But he wasn't. He was exactly the same. Sex had solved nothing. He was just as unsettled, dissatisfied and irritable as he had been the week before.

He'd had sex, but he didn't like the girl. And when the sex was over and the booze had worn off he felt exactly the same as he had before it all began. He had re-lost his virginity and nothing had changed. I suspect he secretly wished he had waited for marriage.

Masturbating Upside Down

One night when I was 13 I orgasmed eight times while watching Maria Conchita Alonso being interviewed on The Arsenio Hall Show. It was a bad idea, a terrible session of teenage masturbation that spiraled out of control, every ejaculation becoming less and less intense until I could barely feel anything and my whole nervous system was in frazzled disarray.

These days I usually masturbate only a few times a week, sometimes just once. I work too much. Most of my days end, not with the satisfaction at having completed a full day, but with an accounting of all the things I didn't get around to that will need to be taken care of later. I've also grown tired of those teenage sessions of whack-attack in my pants. When I masturbate I like to spread out and indulge myself. I like to take my time, and not use any kind of sexual propaganda.

Porn is an easy way to get an erection without having to think about it, but I don't generally use it anymore. It's too distracting and I forget what the point of it all was as soon as I get close to coming. It makes masturbation thoughtless and fast for me. Masturbation is more akin to prison sex than love-making with your one true constant in life. Just think of all the euphemisms for the act that nervous men have constructed for it: beating off, whacking it, pulling the pud, milking the beast, levitating the primate.

There's a bizarre incongruity in imagining the act itself, a frenzied few minutes of knee-buckling friction, and the altar of some airbrushed media construct before which it's generally done. It's like a colony of spider monkeys taking up residence in Versailles and calling it their own.

Since I've forgone the use of porn, my masturbating has become much more focused on positioning. When you're sitting in a chair in front of your computer there's an in-set limit to how creative you can get before you fall over backwards and crack your head on the floor. It's also much easier to think about your whole body when you don't have to fixate on the texture of razor burn and the conspicuous cropping of feet that always pops up in porn. The last time I masturbated I wound up on my bed. With porn I'd have an erection in less than a minute, but lying alone in bed in the middle of the day, with the sound of traffic and the people in the park across the street, it took much longer.

I somehow got into a headstand position on my bed, my feet keeping balance against the wall. This puts a good deal of pressure on the neck and shoulders, but there was something about the rush of blood to the brain in combination with the full body flex I had to maintain to keel over.

I stayed in the position for two or three minutes. I had never been naked and upside-down like that before. It was great. And then I realized I was going to come much sooner than I had thought. I was suddenly in the direct line of fire of my own ejaculate. I had a few seconds to think about what was happening and get into a different position, but I was too taken with the newness of the experience. Then down came the sperm, raining onto my shoulder and comforter, avoiding my face by a lucky few inches, defeated, finally, by gravity.

I Am Error

Maybe you've heard this story already but I'm going to tell it again, because it's mine and I love it.

I met N almost two years ago, on a cold and sunny San Francisco morning. It was Easter and my friend had invited some people over to his apartment for a boozy brunch. As soon as I saw her, before she turned around, I felt like I knew her, and had for as long as I could remember.

Then she turned around and looked at me. I remember thinking it was ridiculous that we were shaking hands and trading names. It should have been a long hug and a 'How have you been?' I thought.

We stayed together the whole day, long after there was any polite reason to. After brunch fizzled out we all went to her place. And then we went to someone else's apartment for a drink. And then we all went to a bar. And then her and I went to another bar. And then we went back to her place again.

I remember finally walking home that night at three in the morning. It had been cold in the afternoon sun, but I felt only a gentle softness in the air of the deserted Mission. We had been drinking since morning but I felt lucid and awake.

We're two totally different people. She's quiet and shy, when I'm spilling over with obnoxiousness. She's direct and assertive where I'd sulk and retreat. She's able to take care of herself where I'd let myself be put out and say nothing. But I understood her instincts, because they were the same as my own. I could read the writing on her wall better than anyone else I'd ever known. It was like knowing what a song's about before you know what the lyrics say. Or like how a dog knows its owner's sad even through its color blindness and inability to speak.

When I decided to move I became an idiot. I decided to move the day after she left, without even knowing it. I was walking across the train tracks to the bus stop after work. The sky was a kind of blue half-dark. I could see a few sad little stars over the flat stretch of industrial rust by the bay. She hadn't asked anything of me when she left, but I thought about what I would have done if she had. Would I have gone with her if she had wanted it?

'No,' I thought to myself. 'That would be the stupidest and most reckless of all options.'

From that point all I could think about was moving, finding a way to make that stupid recklessness real. It was also at that moment that my eventual move stopped being just about her. I never would have moved without her, but I also wouldn't have started off without some self-centered fixation on jumping into the dark holes on the opposite side of 'sensible' and 'safe.' That was my baggage and from that moment forward it was a shadow that followed along behind the body of the act as I put the pieces together.

I told her I had decided to move in a text message a few months later. It was at the end of some teasing exchanges where I'd baited her with barrage of cleverness and verbal ostentation. I didn't want to tell her, but I couldn't help myself, sending it as a self-reflexive cherry on top of the escalating teasing. It's all fun and games until some guy you used to date tells you he's moving across the country for you. It felt like dropping a little lead ball into a black hole when I hit the send button.

She didn't respond. She stopped talking to me for almost two weeks. I was wracked with fear that I had sounded like a jackass. I sent her an email the next morning explaining what I had meant in less priggish language. And still, silence.

She finally called a couple of weeks later, drunk and angry. It was dark and I was waiting at the bus stop on the quiet grassy hill where I'd sometimes see raccoons sprinting across the road. When I saw her name on the phone display a flash of cold went through my stomach. My hands started sweating and my fingers felt swollen and metallic. My blood pressure dropped and my head felt like it was detaching from my body and drifting away into the sky.

'Hello?' I said, already knowing who it was.

There was no small talk. 'Fuck you,' she said. 'Fuck you.'

'Why?' I asked, smiling because I knew already why.

'You're so fucking selfish.'

When I read all of the emails we'd sent each other in the months leading up to that call, I see what she meant. When we met, we fell for each other quickly and recklessly. That's an instinct we both share, the mutual recognition of which helped further our smiling fall. What I don't have is a self-preservation instinct. I was 12 the first time someone punched me in the face, and I didn't understand what was happening. The idea of hitting back or covering up didn't occur to me. My instinct was to step closer and ask 'Why?' And I got hit again.

When she left it was like slamming into the ground after that joyful fall. She was trying to get up and move on. I was still stuck on the ground quietly in pain and trying to manufacture another way to recreate the sensation of falling.

I tried to explain my hedgehog logic to her. My reasons were all stout and low to the ground, they made practical sense. And they all served to point me toward the thing I had wanted to say all along. 'I'm moving for you. I don't want to have felt this and not stood up for it with everything I have,' I told her.

'Fine,' she said. 'Come, I don't care. Write about videogames, make your movies, do whatever you want.'

'I will,' I said.

'Good. Come then.'

Leading up to that moment, I'd tried to be the together one. I fought to not let on how much I was feeling. I never asked her what she thought about the idea. I never included her in my inner debate. And then I announced that I had made a decision, one that was invasive, in her honor but with no consultation in advance. I was moving for her, but at no point had I asked her to have a voice in that decision. I was afraid she'd say no. If she did, then I'd be left alone with an abstract idea of moving across the country. I liked being able to say that I was doing it for her. I was romantic and brave, a swollen projection of my emaciated self (I lost almost 20 pounds in depression after she left).

When I finally got to New York, I was two people at once. I was still afraid of the 'no' I superstitiously expected to find out there in ether. I ignored that fear, while my entire shape contorted around it. I was non-committal and breezy outwardly, while inwardly I was astir with the delusion that there would be something to cling to at the end of this new jump. Who wants to be the thing someone mid-leap clings to?

You know how this story ends: with a 'no' that didn't need saying, I'd crab-walked my way into it before I'd ever even asked a question.

A week before I left, we were chatting about the move. 'I just want to toddle around with you,' she wrote.

'We're gonna toddle, girl,' I replied.

':)'

I've never lived in a place like New York. I wake up every morning with a terrible sense of fear. I have to redefine myself every day to write, to support myself. I don't have the cyclical stability of a job and an office full of people in the same predicament. No one cares that I'm up in the morning. I also feel overwhelmed with some gravitational joy when I walk around the streets. People are everywhere, and they all seem to be heading straight towards me without even looking.

I can see the Empire State building reaching up out of the skyline, lit up in a new color every night. I go rambling down the shady cobblestone streets of the West Village, drink cheap whiskey in East Village bars that smell like ammonia and beer, ride the train to every random part of Brooklyn as if it were another continent. One night I saw Placido Domingo conduct

Verdi, another I danced on a rooftop on St. Marks. I've dated an ex-beauty queen, gone ice-skating at the foot of skyscrapers, and woken up to see snow falling on the tar paper and chimneys on my sunken roof.

I feel lucky to be here. I don't deserve to live in a place so densely filled with this much life, secretly aspirating down the avenues. But I do. I'd wanted this for myself all along, to keep moving, to find a reason to not settle down and grow grass beneath my feet. I wanted to keep pushing against the outer lip of what I can do. I wasn't brave enough to say that I wanted this for my own sake. So I said it was for someone else, and that spared me the terrible weight of having to look at myself without the warping hue of romance.

For that, I managed to lose N. I loved her as if I were a child lost in an airport.

When she was in high school, she wrote 'If you love something, let it go' in Spanish on her bedroom wall. The last time I saw her she held on to me longer than I was expecting. We had spent the late afternoon in the park with some of my friends, and then gone to a bar as the sun was setting. A few more friends were on their way to meet me. She had plans with her own friends in Brooklyn. We'd been having strange outbursts of bickering over the last month, passive aggressive fights I was starting to pick. I didn't want to seem overly clingy in parting so I put my arms lightly around her when we were saying goodbye. I knew I'd been clinging and I forced myself to giver her only a light squeeze.

As I started to pull away she was still holding on. I didn't understand. I stood there with my arms half around her shoulders as she pressed herself against me a few seconds longer.

I looked at her wondering if there was something she had to say. I felt my face warm a little. She lifted her head and looked at me.

'Goodbye,' she said.

Levitating in Time

Is time something we must believe in? The childhood definition still seems good enough, one thing happens after another. It was a skill to learn, keeping things in order, to separate the dusty sandlot where I sat in diapers looking up at a narrow tree trunk from the morning of a birthday (my third) when I hoped the neighbors would bring me a certain kind of toy car made of painted wood. That one should have happened before the other seems nonsensical now. These moments are clearly inseparable, and indeed, they are both happening again, simultaneously, as I look back to them.

There is a beguiling theory of material in the universe that says everything can be traced back its originating point, we only lack the mathematics and measuring tools to complete the computation. Consider an ink drop fallen into a bath and let drift for a few moments. On this shrunken scale, one could, by measuring the speed and angle of every single molecule of ink within the bathwater, retrace their paths and arrive at an exact understanding of the original size of the ink drop, the speed with which it hit the water, and the distance from which it was dropped.

I didn't know how to kiss N that first time in the empty disco, sitting beside her on the red vinyl bench beneath the rotating disco ball, whose light limned the cement floor and the leaky finger of water reaching out from the open bathroom door. I went slowly and she pushed into my mouth, needful and fast-moving. I tried to follow her movements, pressing back harder and widening my lips. I kept opening my eyes, seeing her thick brown hair hanging in front of the glittering flecks on the red bench. It was too distracting to keep them open for long, so I'd close them. Then I'd open them again, amazed that this was happening.

After a few minutes of kissing we decided to walk back to her apartment. On the way, I moved my left hand toward hers and she grabbed it, lacing our fingers together. In her apartment she led me into the dark bedroom. I sat on the foot of her bed and watched her take off her shoes in the long closet that connected her bedroom to the bathroom. The closet let out a small rectangular window of light.

She came back to where I was sitting and leaned down over me, standing between my legs. We kissed again and I wrapped my arms around her lower back, pulling her onto the bed. Her mouth was sour, like old champagne and cigarette smoke. I liked it. Beneath the decay of the day's affections, I could taste her, too, sweet and neutral, the home-like warmth of the air under a blanket after a long night's sleep. I put my hand in her pants and floundered for a few minutes. The tension of the waistline pressed into my forearm. I tried to find some point of arousal in the hedge maze of hair, skin, and moisture. I tried to rub a wide area and hone in on a central point. Her soft moans were inscrutable.

I decided instead to find a small point above her pubic bone and rub in small circles but this too failed to produce any change. I sensed the panic of incompetence coming and put my hand on her back again. I pulled her shirt off over her shoulders. She pulled my shirt off. We kissed again. I grabbed her bra clasp with my left hand and tried to reach my right hand around to help break the tension in the strap. My arm was pinned under her upper ribs and I could only just swipe at the lacy bottom edge.

'Here, let me help you with that,' she said, sitting up again and bending her arms behind her.

As she pulled her bra off I felt a rush of shyness. I wanted to look at her breasts, and yet I didn't want that curiosity to come at the cost of not looking at her face, which was still enough of a mystery after 12 hours. This preciousness sat on top of a quivering uncertainty about just what exactly I was supposed to do with her breasts. Having been thrown by her nethers I thought her breasts were my next best chance, but how to start? I always feel infantile sucking on a woman's breasts, while in just massaging them I begin to suspect I'm underperforming, leaving some other body part unattended.

I put my clumsy hands on both breasts and she lowered herself over me. I tried to rub the hardening nub of her nipples with the center of my palms, pushing them against the fatted ridges of bone below. I rolled on top of her and narrowed my thumb and index fingers around the edge of her nipples, then tightened on the jutting point, pulling it outward. That didn't work either. I felt like I was in a lonely boat, helplessly trying to sound the shape and workings of the woman above me with only isolated sense fragments to guide me.

The penis was my one last move, my six-inch Hail Mary, my golden ticket to whisk us away from the slums of my incompetence. Yet I was terrified that too would fail, worse even than all the others. Even through the marathon drinking and tobacco I was sure it would take me more time to put on a condom than I would be able to last once inside her. Sex would risk revealing the full aspect of my failings. And beyond that I was afraid of how I would respond if we had sex. I had never felt such an immediate gravitational draw to another woman. Adding sex to that experience could either destroy that closeness or else catapult me further into it, like a black hole with no possible escape.

At this point I realized she was snoring. I pushed myself up onto an elbow and looked down at her. Her eyes were closed and her mouth half-open, letting slip a low rumble from her sinuses. I shook her shoulder softly.

'Hey,' I said. 'Are you sleeping?'

A breathy 'ppwahh' came from her mouth . I shook her again. There was no response.

I rolled onto my back next to her, my belt buckle undone and the cold air hitting my chest, running over the warmth her skin had left there. I looked at the alarm clock on her nightstand. It was after 2AM. I would have to wake up for work in four hours, and I was still a 30-minute walk from my apartment. I thought about falling asleep next to her and getting up early to walk home in time to change my clothes and shower. I looked at the ceiling, listening to her breath catch in her throat. I could still taste the sourness of old tobacco in my mouth, hers and mine. I smelled her skin on mine. I would never be able to fall asleep next to her.

I kissed her on the cheek and whispered, 'Good night.'

I stood up, buckled my belt, and pulled my shirt on. I didn't have any way to contact her, we hadn't traded phone numbers or email. We hadn't made any other plans to meet. I looked at her one last time. I thought about finding a pen and paper to leave my number but I knew she would never call me. So I just left. I didn't know what would happen next, but I knew I would find her again, beg her number from our friends, and then – something.

I walked home in the cold night air feeling warm and happy in my shirt sleeves. The Mission was empty but the street lights were bright and filled in the gravelly details along the sidewalk. Two months after I moved to New York, N and I stopped talking and I never thought I would see her again.

After my grandfather died it became clear that my grandmother couldn't live on her own anymore. She had Alzheimer's disease and her mischievous forgetfulness – which in my childhood had been only cover for a conspiracy that always ended with me getting handfuls of illicit candy – was now more serious. The stove would be left on all night. She'd get off the bus at the wrong stop, having forgotten where she was going, and suddenly become lost for hours. One of my grandfather's last wishes had been that she not be put in a nursing home. He was certain her buoyant optimism and playfulness would wither in a place with plastic-wrapped mattresses and the decrepit old bodies who regularly demonstrated their need for such things.

But to the nursing home she went. She lives in a large room, the sleeping area separated from the sofa and television by a tall bookcase, whose shelves are stuffed with a bric-a-brac mirage of old family photos. There's my mother as a baby held up to my grandmother's smiling face, her eyes shining through the emulsion's black and white murk. And right beside, there's my brother's wedding, him and his wife posed in sheeny modern clothing against an incandescent sunset (I remember that sunset, and it was never so bright nor that color). And there I am, hovering on the right wing of a family portrait, face momentarily tricked into a polite smile by some stuffed animal, my parents spry young lovers still, they almost seem grateful for the camera's presence, capturing them in that mysteriously happy condition.

It sometimes feels that my grandmother has abdicated her place in time, as if it were a chair one could just get up from. She has not yet traveled so far from it that my mother and I are strangers. There is sometimes a faint confusion on her face when we come walking down the linoleum corridor, but she never fails to recognize our faces. The names are sometimes confused, and even the relationships—she very often rearranges the seat assignments in her memory's banquet, leaving me at someone else's chair. But there is no question, yet, of who I am to her. Fuck my name, fuck my genealogical title—she still knows me, all the old corners of her brain still fire with the disembodied moments of joy we shared in our candied conspiracies of the past. They seem, in some ways, to have sweetened in her, glazed in the lustrous ink plucked from the thin bathwater of time, and swirled across her subconscious undiluted.

I lived in this way after N left, sickly, willfully surrounded by my memory. I fought against time, stubbornly thinking that I could, through some trick of faith, return again, simply by charging ahead, belligerent and convinced that I could return again to the wholeness and simpleness of the originating drop, just free from its meniscus, falling. It was suicide without the deathwish. I didn't want to stop existing but could not accept that my feelings had so little impact on everything around me. 'It's got nothing to do with you, if one can grasp it,' David Bowie had sung to us the night I drove to her hometown, strolled through her childhood memories, and settled into the near-empty taxidermy bar where the bartender was feeding his pitbull pieces of beef jerky from his mouth, the dog springing to its hind legs to nip them.

In New York she lived a few miles from me. We could have seen each other anywhere. That we went two years in silence and apart was, in fact, an extension of my stubborn insistence that circumstances themselves should change on behalf of my feelings. I mourned, I avoided relationships, I drank, I went out with new women but remained celibate. Every new joy I found connected back to her, shone a light on the ink she'd left in my brain. All of these little prompts to remember her absence were torturous. It was absurd that, when prompted with a song we used to know or a funny experience I knew she'd like, I wouldn't just tell her, send her a text message and let it be that. But I was certain she didn't want to hear from me, and I was doubly certain that all these needful pangs, wanting for some pretext to reach her, to see her name lit inside the screen of my phone, weren't to be trusted. The sour selfishness I'd discovered in myself seemed to lurk behind every impulse to reach out to her. If I couldn't be anything other than a needful burden then I couldn't be anything at all. And so I shut up and stayed apart.

When she finally called me again, almost exactly two years after I came to New York, I squealed like a woman. She sent me a text message first, 'Hey Mike, it's N. I'm curious about your status in life ... are you up for a chat?' If I could have composed the scene in advance I would have wept, but it was mine only to react to, and so I behaved like a small child exhaling high-pitched bursts of air, bouncing on the couch for a moment, then getting up and walking across the living room for no reason whatsoever, then returning to the couch, then squealing some more, and then bouncing again.

I wrote her back in the most restrained spasm of grammar and manners that I could manage, and two minutes later there was her voice again, small and buffeted with sirens and taxi horns as she walked through midtown, but hers, mine, there, again.

And so we shyly, haltingly, quickly became friends again. She had a boyfriend, and was living with him. I still wanted to be her boyfriend, too. I felt little needles of jealousy when he was mentioned, but those acrid thoughts were so much smaller than they had been before, diffuse, diluted, drawn further out from the inky core than they had been.

Six months later, she told me a funny thing: she was breaking up with her boyfriend and moving back to San Francisco. A month after that, she left.

I do not think time can be disbelieved. Our problems with time come from the mystery of its ordering, its consequent actions, one produced from the other. We cannot accept time as a complementary phenomenon producing simultaneous actions, whose threading fingers are so numerous that we only process it in momentary segments. Like a naked body in the dark, we can have some sense of the whole only through insinuation of the moving parts. The hand does not move because of the mouth, but together with it. That naked moment does not precede the departure, the quiet cab ride to the airport, the trunk sagging with the weight of luggage – it happens with it, simultaneously, two spreading limbs from the same drop. If love is a sickness it's one that tricks us into attacking ourselves, spiting one part of the inky corpus because of an irrational fixation on another.

How can this end? As surely as one can trace back the origin of an ink drop one must be able to predict the shape it will create based on its starting point. One could know this, if our math was good enough, our understanding of materials thorough enough, and our measurement tools sensitive enough. One could know, but not here. I love you, N. Loved, love, will love. For here is my blot, the limbs and dreams and memories, suspended in an ocean of time, alive, levitating.

Contemporary culture has eliminated both the concept of the public and the figure of the intellectual. Former public spaces – both physical and cultural – are now either derelict or colonized by advertising. A cretinous anti-intellectualism presides, cheerled by expensively educated hacks in the pay of multinational corporations who reassure their bored readers that there is no need to rouse themselves from their interpassive stupor. The informal censorship internalized and propagated by the cultural workers of late capitalism generates a banal conformity that the propaganda chiefs of Stalinism could only ever have dreamt of imposing. Zer0 Books knows that another kind of discourse – intellectual without being academic, popular without being populist – is not only possible: it is already flourishing, in the regions beyond the striplit malls of so-called mass media and the neurotically bureaucratic halls of the academy. Zer0 is committed to the idea of publishing as a making public of the intellectual. It is convinced that in the unthinking, blandly consensual culture in which we live, critical and engaged theoretical reflection is more important than ever before.